W9-BOD-815

THE LADY GANGSTER

A Sailor's Memoir

THE LADY GANGSTER

A Sailor's Memoir

By Del Staecker

CABLE PUBLISHING

Brule, Wisconsin

THE LADY GANGSTER: A SAILOR'S MEMOIR

First Edition

Published by:
Cable Publishing
14090 E Keinenen Rd
Brule, WI 54820

Website: cablepublishing.com
E-mail: nan@cablepublishing.com

No part of this book may be reproduced or transmitted in any form or by any means, electronic or mechanical, including photocopying, recording, or by any information storage or retrieval system without the written permission of the publisher, except for the inclusion of brief quotations in a review.

© 2009 by Del Staecker
All rights reserved. Published in 2009

Hardcover: ISBN 13: 978-1-934980-21-7
                  ISBN 10: 1-934980-21-8

Soft cover: ISBN 13: 978-1-934980-22-4
                  ISBN 10: 1-934980-22-6

Library of Congress Control Number: 2008933843

Printed in the United States of America

Dedication

For sixteen years I admired my father from a distance. After he shared his Navy experiences with me, I knew that my devotion had been well placed. This book is dedicated to my father—and friend—Irvin Staecker, and all the other heroes who served aboard the USS *Fuller*.

photo courtesy of www.Hyperwar.com

"The saga of 'The Queen of Attack Transports,' begins on the following pages. God blessed all that sailed on her."

– Elgin B. Bowen GM2/c

"We men on the *Fuller* experienced a war not many Navy personnel would."

– Richard R. Hennig BM 1/c

"Mixed in the paint on her decks was the sweat and blood of a lot of boys from Chicago. The *Fuller* was us!"

– Irvin H. Staecker BM1/c

Contents

Acknowledgments

My wife encouraged me to write this book and for that prompting, as well as other assistance, I am forever grateful. Dwight Staecker offered tremendous help with photos and gave me the kind of support that only a really special older brother provides. Former crewmembers Elgin Bowen, Donald Lutes, Sr., and Richard Hennig were tremendous resources. I thank them for assisting with this book and also for their wartime service aboard the USS *Fuller*. Nan Wisherd and Flint Whitlock were superb editors. A special thanks to Red Panda Graphics for the maps and the cover design, Norm Dodge for photo work, and Deb Zime for layout.

Additionally, I wish to thank the helpful staffs of two important museums: the National World War II Museum, in New Orleans, Louisiana, (which displays the only full-size replica of a Higgins boat), and the Air Zoo, in Kalamazoo, Michigan, (which is the home of the National Guadalcanal Memorial Museum).

Foreword

This book is a story of men and a ship, and also the author's homage to his father and relatives from Chicago who made up part of the crew of *The Gangster* (actually the USS *Fuller*) in World War II. The title is the crew's nickname for their ship, and chosen because so many aboard were from Chicago, a city associated with the gangster era of the 1920s and early '30s. The account is soundly based on research in ship records, journals of crewmen, and the memories of the men who served on the vessel. Most of these men were called into active service before Pearl Harbor, and some of them served fully five years aboard the ship. During that time, *Fuller* may have seen as much action as almost any vessel in the U.S. Navy.

Yet this is also a story about a particular kind of ship, the assault transport ship (APA), which, until now, has received relatively little attention from either historians or fiction writers. *The Gangster* started out as a peacetime passenger ship, and, purchased by the U.S. government in 1940, was converted into a troop-and-cargo carrier (and as such, designated AP-14). As events moved the U.S. toward war, the Navy and Marine Corps were already preparing for amphibious assaults that would almost certainly play an important role in its conduct in both the European or Pacific theaters. They understood that the landing craft, carrying the assault troops and their supplies, would require special support ships as floating bases. *Fuller*, and vessels like her, were eventually armed and prepared for the role; an early conversion, she was re-designated as APA-7.

The assault transport ships were armed with 5-inch, 3-inch, and rapid-fire 40mm and 20mm guns, and thus had a measure of self-defense. Each was intended to provide berths, food, medical services, and re-supply to as many as 1,200 troops at a time. After a landing, and when the supplies aboard ship were depleted, such vessels could steam to distant bases for cargo, then return to the beachhead. According to the author, and over the course of the war, the U.S. Navy designated 230 vessels as APAs, and they carried out thousands of missions.

The Gangster played a vital role in the U.S. invasion of Guadalcanal in 1942, the first U.S. and Allied offensive of the Pacific War. In the early weeks after the first landings, she was at times almost alone in re-supplying the embattled Marines ashore. She then served in nearly every landing in the Solomon island chain. She narrowly escaped enemy bombs on many occasions. Over the course of the war, her anti-aircraft fire downed seven attacking aircraft. (A lucky ship, her only serious damage during the war was the result of a collision with a U.S. destroyer.) Some of the most harrowing moments for some of *Fuller's* crew (including the author's father) happened when landing with the early waves of Marines and facing the scathing fire of the Japanese. *Fuller* was present at Peleliu, the most costly of the amphibious assaults in the Pacific relative to the number of Americans engaged; also at Leyte, and finally at the invasion of Okinawa. One of the *Fuller's* captains received the Navy Cross, the second-highest decoration that the U.S. Navy can bestow.

The author expressed the hope that he had done justice to the memory of *The Gangster*, her crew, and, of course, his father. I believe that in this book, he did them far more than just justice; he honored them. In addition, he has furnished his readers with a valuable perspective on the war, the ships, and the men who manned them.

—Larry H. Addington,
Professor of History Emeritus, The Citadel
Author of *The Blitzkrieg Era and the German Staff, 1865-1941*

Introduction

After receiving a degree in history from The Citadel and while pursuing a graduate degree in the same field, I accompanied my father to a Guadalcanal Campaign Veterans Reunion in Seattle, Washington. At that time I promised him I would one day write an account of the Chicago Boys and their amazing five years at sea aboard the USS *Fuller*.

I held off writing for quite a while, always saying—giving the excuse—that the story required formal treatment.

Off and on, again for too many years, I read, conducted research, attended more meetings, and interviewed veterans. I began building a file that would support and, hopefully, produce a traditional historical work. During this time I kept telling myself that the *Fuller's* exploits could only be properly told through detailed professional scholarship. I was wrong.

In the end I came to understand that a story is far more important than the form of its telling. *The Lady Gangster* is a personal tale, and I could only tell it as a story which came about because a son wanted to know more about his father.

A Sailor's Memoir

Chapter 1

0800 hrs, 9 April, 1941

On this chilly Seattle morning, an anxious group of young men stood at the dock's end. Most were not far beyond boyhood. Many were friends, some were relatives, and at least two were brothers. Only a short time before, the majority of these former "Dry Landers" had called the neighborhoods in and around Chicago their home. Now, however, they were dressed as sailors, and their former city life was far behind.

As reservists they had abruptly been called to active duty, and everything in their lives had quickly changed. In January 1941, they were sent to the state of Washington.

After several months of rumor-filled waiting, they found themselves on this particular morning on a dock at Lake Union in Seattle. The familiar sights and sounds of Chicago were indeed long gone. Now life at sea and its adventures lay before them in the form of the newly commissioned vessel they came to board. For many of them this ship would be home for the next five years.

The majority of the assembled sailors were seeing her for the first time. None of the Chicago Boys were experienced enough with ships to be either rightly impressed or disappointed, so they remained quiet. Silently they waited for comments from the older, more experienced men standing nearby.

The other group, to which they would look for leadership, was comprised of experienced petty officers from the regular Navy. Some were actually "old China Sailors" who had served on the gunboats of the Yangtze River and the China coast. These tough, no-nonsense veterans were assigned to teach the new kids how to be real sailors. The inexperienced youngsters understood that the opinions of the "Salts" meant everything. The boys watched as the veterans walked the ship's length, carefully observing her lines.

The ship had received extensive work since being transferred from civilian duty to the Navy. One hundred feet had been added to her hull's length to increase her cargo carrying capacity. To insure that she could quickly move greater loads, important changes had been made below deck. Officially, the new engines could propel her to sixteen knots. But, in fact, she could do better when pushed.

Her speed and toughness would bring many solitary and dangerous assignments in the years ahead. The alterations of her design, the added power, and her unique crew would be important factors in her ability to perform like no other ship. These unique characteristics would help build her reputation as "Queen of Attack Transports."

"Is she fit?" the experienced eyes of the veterans asked. "Oh, yes." The answer was clear to the experienced sailors. "She'll do fine!"

Their next question, "Can these city boys handle her?" would be answered in time.

Chapter 2

The Ship

Officially, she was the USS *Fuller*. During the years of World War II, she would be known by many additional names and designations: AP-14, APA-7, the *Queen of Attack Transports* and the *Old Girl* are but a few. To the battle-tested soldiers and marines of the South Pacific she was *That Glorious Lady*. To her crew, the sailors originating from the neighborhoods of Chicago and its nearby towns, she naturally became known as *The Gangster*.

Originally built in 1919 by Bethlehem Steel Corporation as SS *City of Newport News*, the ship destined to become known as *The Gangster* had been acquired by the U.S. Navy on November 12, 1940, and renamed as USS *Fuller*. As a response to the threat of war, the Navy was rapidly expanding, and a large number of civilian passenger ships and freighters were being converted to military transports. In April 1941, the *Fuller* had just emerged from her makeover at the Puget Sound Navy Yard in Bremerton, Washington, and was designated as AP-14.

The newly acquired ship, renamed USS *Fuller*, as she appeared in 1941 and designated AP-14.

The young sailors on the dock were also part of America's preparations to quickly expand the active-duty Navy. In October 1940, the 20th and 26th Divisions of the U.S. Naval Reserve, based in Chicago, had been alerted for mobilization to man newly acquired ships. On January 2, 1941, sixty-seven officers and 327 enlisted men, some from the old Illinois Naval Militia, were levied for active service. They were sent to Puget Sound to partake in the commissioning of the USS *Fuller*. Some of the reservists were so inexperienced that they actually received their first uniforms just before boarding the train to Seattle. All the sea training of these reservists would be on-the-job under the tutelage of experienced petty officers from the regular Navy.

On April 9, 1941, it would have been impossible to predict what the converted ex-Baltimore Mail Lines ship and its uniquely homogeneous crew would accomplish. Five years and many thousands of sea miles later, *The Gangster* would complete its service shortly following the occupation of Japan and after she had amassed an incredible list of achievements in multiple theaters of war.

Perhaps the story of the USS *Fuller* is best presented in the words of an eyewitness report, filed, in early 1944, by Marine Corps combat correspondent, Staff Sergeant Maurice E. Moran:

Dateline Unknown
—Aboard a U.S. Navy transport in the South Pacific—

Combat planes dip their wings in salute as they pass this ship because they recognize her as a queen with glorious pedigree. She's ploughed through those waters so long pilots regard her as a "landmark." Although old as ships go, she has played a dramatic part in America's war on the oceanic fronts.

Commissioned in 1919 as a cargo-passenger vessel, this transport was re-commissioned as a U.S. Navy vessel in 1941. Since then she has rolled up an unbelievable record of "first in war."

She was in the convoy which transported U.S. Marines to Iceland, the first American troops to land on foreign soil in this global war. When the Japs' sneak punch forced America into the conflict, she helped transport the first American Expeditionary Force to the British Isles. On her return trip she served as a mercy ship, bringing hundreds of bomb-beleaguered British men, women and children to haven in the United States.

Then she sailed into the Pacific.

Out here she became one of the first transports to land U.S. Marines at Guadalcanal. Her tough hide endured a rain of Jap bombs. On her bridge deck are emblazoned four tiny Jap flags, symbols of torpedo bombers who tried to get her and fell before the marksmanship of her crew.

Since the first thrust at the Solomons, the *Queen* has been engaged in a perilous shuttle game, transporting troops and supplies to the area's hot spots and bringing out wounded, sick and prisoners. She's had several close squeaks.

Several times she brought supplies to the Solomon forces on a hit-and-run basis, unloading until the bombing got too hot and then running out of the harbor until the raiders disappeared. Once when the Marines' supplies were virtually nonexistent, the *Old Lady* saved the day by rushing in an overload of dry stores. Every inch of available space was used for food, including holds normally used for troops.

A ship bearing such distinction could be manned only by a gallant crew. Its first skipper, Captain Paul S. Theiss, USN, of Indiana, Pennsylvania, won the Navy Cross for his handling of the vessel in the Solomons. According to William E. V. Stewart, Boatswain's Mate First Class, USN, of Seattle, with the ship in all of her adventures, Captain Theiss is "the fightingest man I ever saw – and our new old man is just like him."

A Sailor's Memoir

Chapter 3

The Attack Transports of World War II

Beginning in 1940, the Navy rapidly expanded in response to the growing prospect of war. A significant number of passenger and freight cargo ships were acquired from civilian sources for conversion into military transport vessels. These ships were given hull numbers in the AP (transport) series.

APs like the *Fuller* (originally designated as AP-14) were named after presidents, signers of the Declaration of Independence, distinguished generals and admirals, famous women, and historic places. The *Fuller* was named in honor of Major General Ben Hebard Fuller, Naval Academy Class of 1889, who rose to become the Commandant of the Marine Corps.

The *Fuller* and some of the other early APs were equipped specifically to handle landing craft in order to participate in and support amphibious assaults. In late 1942, the Navy determined that these amphibious ships were actually a separate category requiring a new designation. To more clearly describe these ships and their capabilities, they received the designation of APA to denote them as attack transports. The re-classification took effect in February 1943, and it was then that the *Fuller* became APA-7.

The *Fuller* as APA-7

9

During an amphibious assault, APAs like the *Fuller* were expected to deliver up to a battalion of troops to a hostile beachhead. The APAs were able to provide berths, food, medical services, and re-supply in support of their human cargo. From an anchored position, as many as 1,200 troops and equipment were delivered by the ship's crew using the landing craft kept onboard. After landing troops, an APA remained near the beachhead to conduct support activities such as re-supply and evacuation. When shipboard stores were depleted, the APAs returned to rear area bases and, as was often the case for the *Fuller*, shuttled supplies and reinforcements in perilous conditions back to the beachhead. During World War II, the Navy designated 230 ships as APAs with six (including early APs so designated) being lost in combat.

More often than not, accounts of war focus upon combat units at the front lines. Regrettably, the heroic actions of other personnel are often overlooked. Long after submarine warfare and air power has forever relocated the edge of the battlefield, logistic and support units are still seen as being non-combat in nature. Brilliant assaults and heroic defensive stands are the remembered highlights of campaigns, not the delivery of troops, ammunitions, and medical supplies. Yet, without the latter, victory in World War II would have been impossible.

The battle-tested attack transports of the U.S. Navy's Amphibious Force were crucial to the effort that wore down the Japanese dream for expansion and empire, and any ship and crew involved in the various campaigns against the Japanese had reason to be proud. However, it may prove impossible to find another ship to equal the service record accomplished by the USS *Fuller* in the Atlantic and Pacific theaters of World War II.

My father, Irvin Staecker, served throughout the war on the USS *Fuller*, and I was awed when I learned of his adventures. Everything I have come to know about the APAs convinces me that the officers and men who served on board them were all heroes. Until now, the world has not known about the *Queen of Attack Transports*, a ship lovingly called *The Gangster*. The USS *Fuller* was indeed the epitome of these amazing ships.

Chapter 4

The Broken Radio – July 1967

For me the story of the *Fuller* began in 1967 when my father pressed me into service. "You'll have to drive," was all he said. He assumed I would understand. My father was like that—he gave orders. I obeyed—reluctantly.

From my view we weren't a particularly tight-knit father and son duo. Our brand of closeness was peculiar to ourselves; nothing like the Waltons. Our expressions of affection were stoic and rare. Always near the surface, love was ready to erupt; spasmodic and somehow beautiful yet frightening due to its unanticipated appearances. We seldom hugged, never kissed. I was almost fully grown before I really knew my father, and if our car radio hadn't broken, I may have missed learning about him entirely.

My father's third bout with a bad heart was the reason he informed me I would be piloting the family sedan eleven hundred miles from Florida to Illinois.

"We're leaving for Blue Island tonight," he added.

It was an announcement, not a request, and definitely not negotiable. I had been drafted for chauffeur duty. My job was to deliver him to Blue Island, Illinois, and our old home which sat two blocks outside of Chicago's city limits. A buyer had finally appeared, and some fix-ups were needed before the sale could be completed. I was also drafted as the repairman. I was not thrilled by either job.

"Can we fix the radio?" was my plea.

"I've barely got gas money," was his reply.

I said nothing in return. My expression said it all. With money so tight, fixing the car's radio was another luxury we'd live without. Sandwiches and warm sodas I could stand. *But no music?*

It was going to be a long trip, a silent marathon. Not a journey, nor an adventure. It was a sentence. Without music, we may be forced to actually talk to each other.

Dad's taste in music leaned toward the classical. He was a self-taught violinist. Classic rock was more my thing. I had taught myself the guitar. Our natures were similar, our expressions worlds apart. On the surface we were different, but our cores were the same. We were equally anxious about the trip. He had his reasons; I had mine.

At fifty, my father's world was rapidly changing. He was trying to keep the pieces from falling apart. At sixteen, my world was forming. I was trying to put something together.

As the middle son I saw myself not as the favorite, so I cut my own path. As a self-made prodigal I was often away from home and almost always alone—I kept my distance. If it had been our choice, my father and I never would have connected. If our bonding was ever to happen, it would require considerable outside influences.

In conducting our affairs, we had begun to bump into each other. We had avoided conflict by avoiding each other. But now we sensed more than just the potential for disagreement during the trip.

We were too alike. We made believe there was nothing to deal with: Everything was fine. I can't say how he actually felt, but thinking about the trip was driving me mad. I was desperate. *Eleven hundred miles and no radio?* I entered the zone beyond desperation and dreaded a music-free cross-country trip with my father more than death itself.

For a brief time two years before, it had looked as if illness might bring us together. Dad's second heart attack required an extended hospital stay for him, and my diagnosis of leukemia landed me on the same floor at the same time. As fellow patients facing serious medical challenges, we were forced to begin to know each other. But we were not comfortable with our forced closeness. We got near one another and then backed off. I knew we made up excuses and remained distant.

Those times were tough for our family of six children and parents. Two of us in the hospital put a strain on finances and relationships. For a while it looked as if both of us were not coming home soon from the hospital, if at all. Eventually we were released on the same day: more circumstantial togetherness. Dad's prognosis was "guarded", meaning his physical activities would be severely limited for quite some time. But my outlook was not as good.

At one point I was given a six-week life expectancy. That was about the time I accidentally overheard the doctors explaining my condition to my parents. In those days, teenagers were not well informed about their situations; special wards and patient advocates came later to healthcare delivery. I became more lab rat than patient, and after being poked, prodded, and jabbed for weeks by less than kind and gentle strangers, I took the medical team's view as a challenge. Being a contrarian paid off—I went into remission.

So two years later, there we were, a pair of unlike men facing different slopes of life. Neither of us suspected that this trip would place us on the level ground that would bring us together.

The first few miles of our trip were unbearable. I recall that we each fiddled with the radio a dozen times. Our taking turns with the knobs showed how similar we were in expressing discomfort with the silence. Finally, Dad spoke. "Anything you want to talk about?"

"Nope."

That was it.

There was more silence and then another tit-for-tat session with the knobs on the useless radio. We were in the same car but miles apart. Maybe it was my desperation that prompted me to change things. Perhaps it was simply that our likeness could divide us no longer. Maybe I finally realized that I really did not know my father and it was time I should.

I asked myself, *who is he?*

I knew the basic information about his life. The tough Depression years had been especially hard for his family. His father's sudden death in 1927 had left my grandmother with four children and five dollars. My father, only nine at the time, was the eldest and became a steady provider. When not in school he worked his childhood away at a variety of jobs. How he found time to learn to play the violin was beyond me. All I knew was that somehow he taught himself.

After high school he passed on a scholarship that would have provided a college education and a teaching career in order to support his mother and siblings. When Dad was twenty, he announced to his family, "I've worked hard and I want some time off." He then spent the following year reading all the books in the local library and practicing his violin. He dedicated the year for self-improvement, took it, and then returned to work. He certainly was different; as much the contrarian as I would later become. Everyone loved him. Under pressure I would have admitted I that did, too.

As I drove I took stock of what I did know for certain. I had heard all the family tales—especially the ones about how he had assumed the role as head of the family when my grandfather died. But there was a large gap in his life—five years during the early 1940s that cast a shadow of secrecy over him. Five years is a lot of time to leave blank. My father's wartime activities were a mystery to me. Maybe if I asked about those years he would begin to fill the void between us. I stared at the silent radio and thought some more.

Like most of the kids in our neighborhood, I was keenly aware that I was the child of a World War II veteran. When I was growing up, it seemed that everyone's father, uncle, or older cousin had served in "the big one," as it was called. No one referred to the men around us as the greatest generation. Why state the obvious? We knew it, or, at the very least, sensed that they had done something special. The war was too big and too recent to ignore.

In the fifties and early sixties you could not have gone long without knowing a lot about World War II. It was everywhere. Movies and television content were full of war stories. Fourth of July parades always had ample veteran contingents, and "What did you do in the war?" was often heard when men of a certain age met for the first time. After that common ice-breaker was uttered, men would share facts about branches, units, and combat theaters.

Veterans and their families were understandably proud of their service records. Sharing information about the war was a common practice. However, I seldom heard my father speak specifically about his wartime experiences.

I knew my father had been in the Navy and that he and my uncle served on the same ship. But I knew little else. Dad had been tight lipped. *Was he hiding something?* He usually remained mute when it came to recounting anything personal. I considered this peculiar since he was in fairly constant contact with his war buddies. I grew up knowing that he and a group of Navy vets from the Chicago area met on a regular basis. *What did they share? Why did I not know more?*

For years after our memorable auto trip, I researched the exploits of my father's ship, the USS *Fuller*. An account in the local newspaper shed some light on his silence. The 1944 article was meant to boost the morale of war-weary citizens. My father was home for the first time in two-and-a-half years, and the homefolks were justifiably proud.

The headline of the *Blue Island Sun Standard* read:

"IN NAVY 3 YEARS – IRVIN STAECKER ON FURLOUGH."

However, the reporter must have been sorely disappointed when he only could write, "Irvin doesn't talk for publication about his experiences—he has seen too much to talk. He knows the value of silence."

A broken radio and eleven hundred miles of highway provided the key to unlock those five years of his life. But only because I stopped staring at the radio and ventured to ask, "Dad, will you tell me what you did in the war?"

I cannot say with any certainty what I expected to hear from my father. At first he said nothing. I assumed he was going to keep silent. As we continued driving north toward Illinois, I glumly stared at the bugs decorating our windshield. I was miserable and was certain my father knew it. I thought he was going to ignore my question, remaining distant in his silence, but my father surprised me.

After what seemed an eternity, he began to talk. He spoke softly, in a conversational tone and manner new to me. Occasionally I asked a question, but for the better part of the next eighteen hours my father shared the exploits of the ship known as *The Gangster*.

A Sailor's Memoir

Chapter 5

War Looms During Hard Times – August 1940

I enlisted over a year before our country entered the war. It was August 1940. Oh boy! Was your grandmother upset! But she wasn't mad at me. She was furious with your Uncle Art and our cousin Al Schaller. They were the reasons I joined the Navy.

Cousin Al was already in the Naval Reserves and had sold Art on the idea of enlisting. Al convinced Art that America was entering the war no matter what and that joining early was the smart thing to do. Your uncle was just seventeen and enlisted without anyone else in the family knowing. Mom's anger was understandable. She had been a widow for over ten years and had run our household alone. In your grandmother's way of thinking, Cousin Al had stolen one of her children.

Al had personally escorted Art to the Naval Armory at the foot of Randolph Street in downtown Chicago and witnessed his signing up. I'm pretty sure he got some special recognition for his recruiting effort. When Mom found out, it was too late. I never saw her so mad. Her solution to Art's enlisting was unexpected: She specifically told me it was okay to consider enlisting, too. It really meant she wanted me to look after my younger brother.

Mom was firmly opposed to the war and any form of military service, but she thought that our being together might provide some form of added protection. Even with that thought, it was still difficult for her to condone, let alone encourage, my enlistment.

Your grandmother did not have much formal education, but she kept up on things. She rarely read the newspaper, but she had a habit of seeking opinions from all sorts of people. She could be rigid and stubborn about most things, but only after careful consideration. She was strongly against the prospect of another war and hated the thought of any one of her three sons being involved. It was no small thing when she "told" me it was okay to enlist.

In 1940, war was already a reality in Europe and China. But in America, people favored isolation. The Depression was still lingering, and few people wanted our country involved in another overseas conflict when there was so much to be done at home. After a lot of tough years, Americans dreamed of peaceful lives filled with work, home, and family. "It's not our fight," was what most people were saying.

Other than work and attending church, your grandmother never had time to be involved with anything, except the Mothers' Crusade. In 1940 she joined over 50,000 mothers from across the country in several anti-war protests. The mothers sought to keep us out of the war in Europe. They also wanted President Roosevelt to promise the impossible—that he would keep their sons out of a war no matter what. The President promised but it was to no avail. Events were rapidly pushing us toward involvement.

In mid-August 1940, the German Luftwaffe launched a thousand-plane raid on the British Isles. The Battle of Britain appeared all but lost as the Third Reich pounded the British. Public opinion began to shift. At heart we all knew that my cousin was right: War was coming. America could not let Britain go under. I took Mom's "advice" and enlisted that week. I never looked back.

Two decades after hearing the previous story, I was visiting my uncle and he shared his version of the Staecker enlistment saga. Uncle Art's version confirmed what I had been told and also provided additional information. Here is Arthur Staecker's account of how he and then his brother joined the Navy:

Your father took a few days to think things over. Our cousin Al gave him the same speech that he gave me, but out of your grandmother's range of hearing. Al was quite a salesman. My enlistment and the idea of us serving together was an added feature in his pitch to your dad.

Although I never actually heard your grandmother tell Irv to join, I suspect she allowed it to happen because she wanted your father to go with me. She naturally saw him fulfilling his role as the eldest son. Your Uncle Vernon also was interested, but your grandmother vetoed his involvement. She said two of her boys serving was more than enough. In those days a lot of brothers served on the same ship. In fact, when the Arizona went down at Pearl Harbor, there were over a dozen pairs of brothers lost on that ship alone.

As I said, Al was pretty good at delivering his recruitment speech, and several of our friends from Blue Island also joined. Jimmie Wilson, Ben Bradford, and Don Smyth also enlisted and served on the Fuller with us.

THE LADY GANGSTER

One Sunday, after attending several Reserve meetings, I clearly remember your father and me stretched out on the front lawn staring up at the clouds of late summer. We shared our impressions of the training and talked about the future war. I jokingly told your father that by joining early we'd be admirals by the time the war was all over. Ever the realist, your father told me I had to be dreaming. He reminded me that the Navy found us so unimpressive that they had yet to provide us with seamen's uniforms, much less those for admirals. We both laughed and continued talking until dusk when your grandmother called us in to supper.

We were young and as green as green could be.

A Sailor's Memoir

Chapter 6

From Pretend Sailors to Almost the Real Thing –
September 1940 to March 1941

My father was a good storyteller and I had often observed him explain things through parables and tales. It was his favorite method of communication. I was pleased to be his sole audience, so I eased into my driving duties and listened.

America was not ready for war, and the Naval Reserve clearly showed how poorly prepared we were as a nation. Our first drills at the Naval Armory were unimpressive. We did very little that would have instilled confidence in our abilities.

In 1940, America's military was undermanned and supplied, if at all, with worn and obsolete equipment. It wasn't anything like today. We had great potential, but you never would have guessed it by seeing us at the Naval Reserve Armory in Chicago.

When our cousin recruited us, his uniform looked sharp and professional. I never had a uniform of my own until the day before we left for Seattle in January 1941. It was only then that they issued uniforms and told us to go home and pack. It was on the train heading for Seattle that I learned how to at least dress like a sailor. We had a few experienced older guys who showed us the proper way to tie a neckerchief and fold our uniforms for travel in our sea bags. Most importantly, they showed us how to wear our hats.

I learned there were very important unwritten rules for wearing a sailor's cap. The code was subtle and served as the means to designate our status. A hat cocked slightly too much could get you into trouble. You never assumed the right to tip it "just so" on your own. You had to be accepted by the "Old Salts"—the experienced sailors of the regular Navy. They were the ones to adjust your cap at a formation or inspection. When they dipped or pinched your cap for you, it was the sign that you were okay. Earning their approval was everything.

"We were young and as green as green could be." January 4, 1941, was a cold day when Irvin Staecker, left, and his brother Arthur proudly posed in their just-issued uniforms before the gates of Memorial Park in Blue Island, Illinois. They departed for Seattle and life at sea later that day.

At that point I asked my first specific question about his experiences. "If you joined in August 1940, what did you do without a uniform for five months?" He laughed. At first I thought it was at me, but his answer explained his mirth.

Well, believe it or not, I swam and dived for the Armory's aquatic team, and your Uncle Art played volleyball. We joked about being professional athletes. The pay came to thirty-four dollars a quarter for attendance at one drill each month.

Like I said, America was not ready for war. Remember, this took place over a year before the attack on Pearl Harbor. We basically just showed up. Each drill was the same. We'd have a reporting formation followed by a brief lecture in one of the classrooms. We had no equipment. The classroom topics were well intended, but we got little out of them without equipment to work on. Navy Pier on Lake Michigan was nearby and there were a few old ships docked there, but other than going on board a couple of times, we were just pretending to be sailors.

The most important and lasting benefit of our time at the Armory was building camaraderie. We knew that eventually we were going somewhere, and most likely together. Later on we realized and appreciated our closeness in being volunteers from the Chicago area. It paid off big once we were aboard the Fuller. *We were pretty much alike, we thought the same, and it helped us in working together. Because of our common background we were a tight-knit group and, when we got to our ship, we quickly became a good crew because of it.*

I couldn't help but think about my own circle of friends being placed under similar stress in such an environment—would we bond as naturally? Vietnam was a dark shadow looming over my generation, and it was then that I realized my father had successfully faced something similar. I listened with even greater focus as he continued.

It was late in October when we were placed on alert. It meant our departure for active duty would come soon. The Navy was expanding rapidly— and calling up units—and we were told to expect orders immediately after Thanksgiving. However, we stayed home until just past New Year's Day. Spirits were high as we left the Naval Armory. It was on the evening of January 4, 1941, that we boarded a train headed west. For many of us, it was the first time away from Chicago, and we had no idea what to expect.

Years later, I came into possession of my father's journal which was aptly entitled *Spray-Days*. His description of the departure was brief and matched his memory:

> We all sang on the bus riding to the depot. We left on time and the train looked strange under the station roof. After riding for an hour and singing more songs to a "Squeeze box" [a small accordion] we pushed into our bunks. Mine was lower #6. Was it cold out and our car (4) didn't heat up so well. Artie froze a little, but nothing serious.

By this time I was extremely interested in listening to Dad's story and had long forgotten about the radio. As I drove he resumed his tale:

The trip west took several days and was a great sightseeing experience. Dining car food proved good, and the service was fit for a king. I recall that our routine of eating and sitting followed by more eating and sitting was only broken up by pointing out the sights and playing cards. Spirits were still high on January 7th when we reached our destination.

Again, from his journal:

> Tues. Jan. 7, 1941. This was the morning we all were waiting for, "Seattle!"

Later, when I was able to examine his journal and compare it with my notes, I was amazed at how good my father's memory was almost thirty years after the events he described. Driving was a breeze as I continued to listen.

Chow that morning was early to allow time for an inspection where everyone looked neat and clean. There were no incidents to report and an officer meeting the train congratulated us on our good conduct. I suppose he expected something different from three hundred "Chicago toughs." I recall it was then we first received that form of recognition. It no doubt planted the seed for the Fuller's nickname as The Gangster.

We did not stay in Seattle for long. That afternoon, in poor conditions, we crossed Puget Sound on the Navy tug Challenger. Our destination was the receiving station in Bremerton. It was my first experience at sea, and it was wonderful to experience Puget Sound clearing from the fog and mist. I regretted knowing then that my future duty assignment was that of a fireman. After that brief experience, I wanted to be on deck forever.

The following three weeks at Bremerton flew past quickly. All I can remember is that Art and I were always assigned to the same work details. Mostly we did clean-up and janitorial work at the primary location for all the community events—the Craven Center. Mom was happy when she read our letters home. Her plan for us being together seemed to be working...until I caught the measles.

What was normally a child's disease laid me low for quite a spell. When I was released from the hospital in mid-February, I learned that I might be reassigned as a deckhand and Art was to be a torpedo man. My assignment made sense. There was a shortage of deck personnel, and I was thrilled at the possibility. But Art's assignment puzzled us. We had been told we were headed for transport duty. What would a torpedo man do on a transport? Was he going to a different ship? Mom's plan was in jeopardy.

When Art's assigned duty was explained it restored our faith in Navy reasoning. We were both going to be assigned to the same ship—a transport of some type. At times transports would naturally be called on to move torpedoes. It made sense that someone on board would understand torpedoes as cargo, not weapons. So Art became a torpedo man.

Your uncle fared well in his assignment. He excelled at book work, having finished high school at sixteen. Art loved to study, and his new rating involved a different form of learning than that of "the deck." For me, a future with a bosun mate's rating was perfect. My duty would be "up top and in the weather." Like many others familiar only with the flat land of the Midwest, I had already fallen in love with open water. I wanted to be a real sailor in the traditional image.

My wish seemed to be fulfilled completely when I learned that I was being sent to San Diego for special training in small boat seamanship. Since Art's new rating required schooling that was not yet available for him, he was also being sent to learn as much as possible about diesels. Mom's plan seemed to be working for us again.

From his journal:

> Monday, February, 24, 1941 - Had a swim tryout for surf boat school at San Diego. Passed and we already (k)new about going so we just lashed out the hammocks and left at 6:30 to board the *Nevada*.

My father's voice showed real joy when he recounted his first time on a battleship. I was able to recreate some of that feeling again for him immediately following the reunion meeting that we attended years later. At that time we drove to Bremerton, his first duty station, and toured the battleship *Missouri*. That shared experience never would have occurred if the radio had been playing during our long drive in 1967. While driving and listening, I sensed that he and I were drawing closer. I encouraged him to continue with his story.

Only battleships are named for states. The Nevada *was huge and we were thrilled to be aboard, even as passengers. The trip south was my first real look at "the regulars" while they worked. They knew their stuff and I was impressed. On our way to San Diego we docked at Long Beach and jumped at the chance to go aboard an aircraft carrier—the* Saratoga. *Traveling on a battleship and visiting a carrier made us feel like sailors. I couldn't wait to start my training.*

We spent most of March in San Diego. I was thrilled to be there. We were learning the basics of handling a new type of landing craft, the LCP [Landing Craft Personnel], better known later as the Higgins boat. At the time I had no idea how important the experience would be. I don't think any of us new guys had a clue about how special these boats were and the role they would play in the war.

I was just glad to be designated a coxswain and "skipper" of my own boat. Artie was my motorman, and we had other sailors with us as deck hands. Although we were supposed to learn each other's tasks, I handled the boat almost all the time because I "had the touch" for the helm.

At that point in the story my father told me that he and the other men from the *Fuller* were actually assigned the very first Higgins boats. I took it as gospel then, but over time wondered how accurate my father's memory could be about such an important detail. I later learned how good his memory was. The LCPs were the initial version of the Higgins boat but not yet equipped with the drop ramp bow so familiar after 1942. His journal entry for describing the newness of the experience with these craft for the Navy, as an institution, does support his claim.

From his journal:

> Thurs., Mar. 6, 1941- No one seemed [to know] w(h)ere to put us or what to do, as this was a new thing with the Navy these "Surf Boats". We finally broke in several new ones.

For crew members of attack transports, maneuvering a fully loaded Higgins boat was a critical skill.

Again, his journal entry of March 10, 1941:

> Warmed up and broke in some new 36 ft. boats. The Captain
> of the Yard growled at a squad we were in and seemed like
> a busy old man out of patience with us all. Then he went off
> telling us not to eat all the chicken and orange juice in the
> Mess Hall. We took out in the boats and had a swell ride all
> afternoon in and out of the buoys and crossing each other's
> path of spray.

March 11th's entry reveals by its tone that all the classes were not
perceived as being of high quality:

> We were given an "instructor" and had the privilege to ask
> and be shown anything pertaining to diesels.

In a short amount of time my father and his fellow sailors must have
been fairly good at handling the Higgins boats. By March 17th they were
allowed to break in more boats as his journal for that day explains:

> Early morning no work and then the afternoon changed. We
> took in six new boats and prepared them for use.

As we drove along I listened intently as he continued: *After several
weeks we were pretty good with the new boats and were a bit surprised to be
sent back to Bremerton. When we arrived in Washington, the word was that
we were soon going to be billeted to a ship. Rumors flew everywhere, and
several names had been mentioned since we left Chicago, but the one most
heard was that of the USS* Fuller.

Early in April, we re-crossed Puget Sound to indeed board the Fuller.
*She was docked at Lake Union in Seattle. At first sight, I did not know what
to make of my ship. My bubble didn't burst, but it definitely lost some pressure. The* Fuller *was not the sort of ship that was on recruiting posters. She
was not exactly ugly. To me she was just very long and grey. She was still*

being worked on and had some rough spots.

Up to that point in my very brief Navy career, I had learned to keep my mouth closed. You watched the veterans and listened to their chatter. My heart pounded as they looked her over. They seemed pleased. Their okay of our new home caused me to stand a bit taller during the on-deck address given by our Commanding Officer.

Captain Theiss was a four-stripe Navy officer, one rank below an admiral. He was regular Navy and a graduate of the Naval Academy. His assignment to the Fuller *was proof that no matter how unimpressive she looked, this ship was important. Only battleships, carriers, and heavy cruisers warranted similar ranked leadership at the top. As the formation broke up, I heard one of the veterans say that he was glad to be on board a "real Navy ship."*

For some reason, from that day forward I knew that my time in the Navy would only be on the Fuller. *I felt linked in a way I cannot explain. I just knew that whatever happened to that ship would somehow also happen to me. I served on her before, during, and after the entire war. She was my ship.*

A Sailor's Memoir

Chapter 7

First Date – April 9, 1941

The next several weeks were really busy. Every day, civilian workmen were still coming on board to complete the final details of the Fuller's conversion. The crew was assigned to cleaning and rigging the ship to get underway. In between work details the petty officers began our practical instruction on how to crew a real ship. We learned new terms—Navy terms—like divisions, details, watches, and gangs for groups of men and hatches instead of doors, overheads for ceilings, and all manner of decks. The Fuller was much bigger and far more complex than I had first imagined, and if it was to be my world, I needed to know a great deal about many new things. I was quickly reminded that my San Diego experience, no matter how good, was all too brief and only with Higgins boats.

I was impressed when my first training session was punctuated with a threat. It reminded me of the fact that I (and many of my pals from Chicago) had not received even the most basic of training—Navy boot camp.

The Chief Bosun grunted, "I'll make sailors out of everyone of you, or YOU'LL DIE TRYING! One day you'll be called an 'Old Salt' by some green boot-recruit and you'll owe that compliment to me."

I never worked so hard in my life. Not only were we getting everything prepared for the Fuller to be seaworthy, we were also trying to absorb vast amounts of day-to-day practical knowledge. There was lots of work and plenty to learn. At the end of each day we fell exhausted into our bunks only to be roused to start another day of equally hard work. The best part of all the effort came on Easter Sunday when I was informed officially that I was no longer a fireman and had been re-assigned as a seaman. I was glad to be a real sailor at last.

"Is that when you learned the knot?" I had to interrupt. When I was a Boy Scout, my father taught me how to quickly tie a bowline knot. Normally, it's one of the simplest knots to learn, but it can take a few moments to complete. My father's version, the flying bowline, was lightning quick in its execution and excellent for use on a boat or in a docking situation.

Yes, one of the China sailors taught us how to tie it, even while running along the deck. It's an "Old Salt" knot. We were docking once and I grabbed a line that was thrown to me. I flipped my wrists and the guy on the dock couldn't believe his eyes. I looped the line over the deck cleat and that was it! He wanted to know how I did it. "Magic," was what I told him.

I won several competitions and a few campground bets tying the flying bowline as a Boy Scout. My asking about the knot did not slow down his comments on being a new deckhand. He went on with his story.

My permanent assignment to the deck quickly changed my outlook on everything. I started to think in nautical terms and was constantly aware of the slightest change in the weather. And this happened before we left the dock for the first time. Some of the guys liked being protected below deck, but I wasn't one of them.

It's strange, but I started thinking of them as passengers on my ship. I know we were all part of the same close-knit crew, but for me, being in the Navy meant more if I worked close to the water. Later there were times when being a Bosun's Mate would put me in danger and I'd see and do things that scared me, but I never ever regretted starting out as a deckhand.

I had always seen my father as a grown man, with skills and abilities based upon his experience. It was strange to hear him speak of a time when he was a "newbie," just learning about life. I wondered how I'd respond in similar circumstances, and most importantly, if I would match his record. It was at that moment that I connected with my father in a profound way—I saw us as equals divided by time. My interest in his words heightened.

As always, rumors of our putting to sea were constantly thick and wrong. As the inexperienced members of the crew, we new guys expected several days of local maneuvers in Puget Sound to take place before our maiden voyage. This seemed to be the case when we moved across the sound to Port Townsend on May 1st. But on May 2nd, we were totally surprised when we left the dock for our anticipated sea trials and just kept on going. There would be no sea trials. We were on our way.

That's how I first learned about the Navy's policy toward announcing departures. Ships seldom left when expected. Rumors were floated as a means of protection. The veterans took it all in stride and soon we would, too. We were underway and our maiden voyage would include all forms of trials and shake-downs. Rumor again had us headed to San Diego. We made our way north through Puget Sound and then west to the Pacific by way of the Strait of Juan De Fuca.

When our bow pointed south the rumors, this time, seemed validated, but I didn't care. I was too busy learning the ropes. On deck we were constantly involved in some activity—securing lines, checking secured lines, re-checking our checking, and keeping watch for anything being out of place or loose. The veterans constantly supervised our every move and corrected mistakes. Nothing was left to chance. From its very beginning the Fuller was run by regulation, experience, and hard work. She was a tight ship—very professional and smooth running. Just like that veteran had observed on the first day, the Fuller was indeed "a real Navy ship."

At one point during the voyage I was ordered to the bridge. I was excited to be there since we were underway, but feared that maybe I was in trouble of some sort. I was relieved when I was instructed to stand behind the helmsman and closely watch as he "drove the ship."

It was there, on this first visit to the bridge, that I began to really understand and appreciate the beauty of a ship at sea. The chain of command, the orders from the Officer of the Deck, the confirmation of orders, the process, and the reports—it was a wonder to behold. Everything made sense from the bridge. Later I learned that my stint as a coxswain had earned me notice as a potential member of the bridge's contingent. I was placed there to absorb the environment, and I did. I drank it in.

From my father's journal:

> May 1-8, 1941 – Had my first wheel watch coming down, a little nervous at first but enjoyed the thrill though. It was at night.

For a few minutes he said nothing. I looked over and knew that he was definitely somewhere else. He caught that I was looking at him and then explained his silence by continuing: *Several years later I vividly remembered the experience of standing behind the helmsman for my training*

The USS *Fuller* (as AP-14) departs Lake Union in Seattle, Washington, on May 6, 1941, and begins its incredible journey of adventure.

on that first cruise. On that later occasion we were making our way across a particularly dangerous area in the Solomon Islands and a different green seaman was on the bridge. He was standing behind me, having also been instructed to watch the helmsman drive the ship. I hoped he was absorbing it like I did.

He went silent again. I didn't want him to stop so I asked the most obvious question I could imagine. "Dad, on the first trip at sea did you ever get seasick?"

He came back vigorously. *Who, me? Never! I was a natural born sailor. Or, at least that's how I remember it. You see, I was up on deck most of the time. The old vets helped us new deckhands get through the worst of it. They told us to watch the horizon and avoid going below unless we absolutely had to. The guys below deck, they really suffered on that first cruise. They paid dearly for getting an indoor rating. But, by the time we hit the waters of southern California, everyone pretty much had their sea legs. We soon passed by Catalina Island and were in port at San Diego on May 6th.*

At San Diego we were assigned to the Base Force of the Pacific Fleet and in less than a week were actively training at sea as part of Pacific Fleet Exercise Number One. From May 13th to the 16th we took part in the first amphibious maneuvers conducted by the U.S. Navy using the new Higgins boats. Our previous experience came in handy as we practiced landing troops on San Clemente Island. A number of heavy cruisers and destroyers followed up the mock landing with bombardments.

There were also several similar transports off the island using the new landing boats. We appeared to have an edge over them, and I think it may have been because the Fuller *was the first transport to have Higgins boats assigned. Things went well and we Chicago Boys were proud of ourselves. Reality set in when one of the veterans reminded us that nobody had been shooting at us.*

A Sailor's Memoir

Chapter 8

Mr. Higgins Built a Boat

At this point it would be beneficial to pause for an examination of the Landing Craft Personnel (LCP) better known as the Higgins boat. The later, and better known version, (the LCVP) was the LCP equipped with a drop-ramp bow.

This craft plays an important role in recounting the exploits of *The Gangster*, and its impact upon the war cannot be overstated. The LCP/LCVP was the product of a truly amazing boat builder—Andrew Jackson Higgins.

Prior to the war Higgins was designing and building shallow-draft wood boats for use in the Louisiana bayous and swamps. Higgins' unique design concepts were highly regarded by the oil industry for use in exploring for drilling sites. It has also been said that the design's origin went back to Higgins' association with rum-running during Prohibition. True or not, Higgins possessed a genius for design that was matched by his blunt approach to business and life.

As good as his design later proved to be, it was slow to find a home with the Navy, perhaps due in part to Higgins' quote that "the Navy doesn't know one damn thing about small boats."

Higgins did not allow anything to stop him once he was focused upon a goal. Certain that there would be a war and the U.S.A. would need wooden boats, Higgins bought the entire 1939 mahogany crop from the Philippines and stored it for future use. It was this type of thinking that brought Higgins and his design to the attention of Marine General Holland (Howlin' Mad) Smith, the father of modern U.S. amphibious warfare, who championed Higgins' cause.

It has also been reported that then-Senator Harry Truman urged the conduct of a head-to-head test between Higgins' prototype and a design from the U.S. Bureau of Ships. In heavy weather, Higgins' boat exceeded all proposed requirements while the Bureau's contender sank. The LCVP was clearly superior to any craft previously employed for the role of delivering supplies and troops to shore from an anchored ship. The

Higgins boat's advantage was due in part to the use of the strong and relatively light mahogany instead of steel.

Some facts about the Higgins boat:

1. The 36'3" by 10'10" wooden craft was powered by a six-cylinder Gray Marine Diesel engine capable of delivering up to 225 horsepower to a single propeller which would move the craft and up to 8,000 pounds of men and supplies as fast as 9 knots (9.9 mph).

2. Some later versions reached as high as twelve knots (13.2 mph) using 250 horsepower Hall-Scott gasoline engines.

3. The propeller was recessed in a tunnel, protecting it from contact with rocks, reefs, and sand bars.

4. It had a shallow draft, drawing only three feet at the stern, two feet amidships, and an incredible two inches at the bow. This feature allowed the boat to approach the shore and drop its bow ramp onto the beach.

5. Light armor was placed on the bow ramp and rearward to the coxswain's station. Armor plating normally consisted of quarter-inch steel and was effective only as protection from small-arms fire.

6. The boat was usually defended by two .30 caliber machine guns and at times was refitted with a .50 caliber.

An optimum crew of four was comprised of a coxswain, a motor mechanic, and two crewmen who served as gunners and manned the fore and aft hooks that were used to raise and lower the boat into the "mother ship." At times the crew was reduced to three members by deleting a deckhand. In those instances the motorman also served as a gunner.

On board the transports, Higgins boats were carried on deck and when needed they were lowered unloaded into the water by deck cranes also called davits. Once in the water, they were filled with supplies by crane or loaded with up to thirty-six troops. Troops boarded the lowered craft by way of netting draped down the side of the ship. Loaded or filled boats moved into a circular staging formation near the ship until enough boats were available to constitute an assault formation, or wave.

The Higgins boat became the primary delivery vehicle for amphibious assaults.

Most of the conversations I had with my father concerning *The Gangster* included comments about Higgins boats and their crucial role in amphibious operations. Getting assault troops and their supplies to the beach and returning the wounded was an attack transport's primary purpose. The Higgins boats were an extension of the ship itself. You could not understand one without the other.

The LCVP was not the only boat designed by Higgins. There was the LCM, a larger landing craft used to land tanks and artillery, and the famous PT boats. But the LCVP earned and kept the Higgins name due in part to its ubiquity. By the war's end, Higgins and twenty-one other licensed manufacturers had produced 23,398 of these remarkable craft. At one point, 92% of the entire U.S. Navy's flotilla was comprised of various craft designed by Higgins.

A great deal more can be said about Higgins and the immense importance his genius in design and construction had upon the war effort. I suggest that anyone interested in learning more about the man and his work visit the National World War II Museum in New Orleans. At this superb museum one can view a perfect full-scale reproduction of an LCVP. In my view, the Higgins boat played a role in American history greater than other famed transportation vehicles such as the Conestoga Wagon and the Yankee Clipper.

If the measure of a man is set by the stature of his foes and admirers, then Andrew Jackson Higgins may be history's most unique character based upon the following:

General of the Armies and President Dwight D. Eisenhower said of Higgins: "He is the man who won the war for us. If Higgins had not designed the LCVP, we could never have landed on an open beach. The whole strategy of the war would have been different."

And Adolph Hitler called Higgins "the new Noah," firmly expressing his belief that Higgins' design changed the world.

My father was not as lofty a commentator. However, his opinion was based upon extensive first-hand experience with the Higgins boat in combat situations. His view was always offered with immense respect. On more than one occasion, I heard him say, "Higgins built one hell of a boat!"

Chapter 9

Scuttlebutt and Secret Orders

We had long since left Florida and were traveling north through Georgia. My father's story had me hooked. I kept driving, skipped eating, and sipped on lukewarm colas to stay alert. I wanted to hear more and pressed him to continue. "Dad, what happened next?"

He had that look again and I knew he was back in May of 1941. He resumed his story.

People say women gossip, but you haven't seen anything until you live on a ship. Sailors are world-class gossips. You get a bunch of sailors and every couple of minutes there's a new rumor or a rehashed version of an old one. If you wanted to, you could spend all your free time chasing scuttlebutt. Scuttlebutt was the Navy's slang for the gossip mill.

Most scuttlebutt is contradictory, confusing, or just plain wrong. The buzz begins when someone hears a bit of news and passes it on. The next person passes on what they heard and so it goes. Pretty soon the original bit of information is so twisted and garbled that the message passed on is whatever the teller slants it to be. A good piece of scuttlebutt can get a life of its own and pass through the network over and over. Each time through it gets changed till you can't recognize it, or the truth.

Toward the end of May we started to hear a great deal about secret orders and a "big move." The scuttlebutt was constant. One of the deck petty officers kicked the rumor mill into high gear after we were given a special painting job. He said we were definitely headed up north.

Almost overnight, we quickly covered the entire ship's light shade of battleship grey with another color. After dark the Fuller was nearly invisible due to the hue of the very dark blue paint we used. The ship appeared black at night. The intent was clear—we were indeed headed for northern waters.

Events at first seemed to confirm the rumors when we loaded units from the 6th Marines. We assumed we were going to Alaska or some other northern spot in the Pacific. With their equipment and supplies stowed, we left San Diego on May 31st with our sister ships the Biddle and the Heywood. Rumors were thick, and we were really confused when we headed south under the protection of several escorts. That's when I decided never to put much faith in scuttlebutt. We wound up in Panama!

The *Fuller's* interim destination was the last entry in my father's journal for almost a year's time. He later told me that due to security concerns and the effects of rumors, the *Fuller's* crew was instructed to stop keeping journals and diaries. In June 1942, the ban was lifted, or perhaps ignored, and my father's note-keeping resumed. However, the last lines on Saturday, June 1, 1941, were:

> Left San Diego and wondered where the *Fuller* was headed. "Panama," hotter than Hades and something we didn't expect to see.

"Panama? Were you surprised?" I asked.

He smiled and continued: *Yes, I was. So much for rumors being right. Real fast we went through the Panama Canal and next thing we "heard" was that we were going to assault the French-held island of Martinique and expel the locals who were loyal to the Vichy government. That proved wrong when we quickly steamed through the Caribbean. We were headed up the east coast of the U.S. in a hurry.*

Although we were not yet in the war, we were always on the lookout for German subs. The same rumors that put us in Martinique next had us fending off the Nazis. That bit of scuttlebutt proved wrong, too.

After five or six days out of Panama, we pulled into Charleston, South Carolina. We were surprised at the number and variety of transports we found anchored there. Whatever we were going to be involved in, it was not going to be a small operation.

We got liberty in Charleston but didn't enjoy it due to the intense summer heat. After a week in port, we transports left in a group with some destroyers serving as escorts.

Our course out of Charleston shows how scuttlebutt can be totally off by being partially right. We did indeed head north, as first rumored back in San Diego. And, we kept going north until we reached Canadian waters. On June 27th we arrived in Placentio Bay, Newfoundland. The West Coast scuttlebutt had the right direction, but the wrong ocean!

It was supposed to be summer, but it was cold in the Canadian waters. We were not used to it and we shivered as we looked at the size of the force we were joining. It definitely convinced us that something big was happening. The formation we had traveled in was only a portion of a much larger convoy.

On the 1st of July we sailed from Newfoundland with many more transports and auxiliaries. For protection we had twenty destroyers, two cruisers, and two battleships, the USS New York and USS Arkansas. It was a serious operation. When we headed northeast, into even colder waters, the rumors really began to fly. Scuttlebutt said we were part of an invasion.

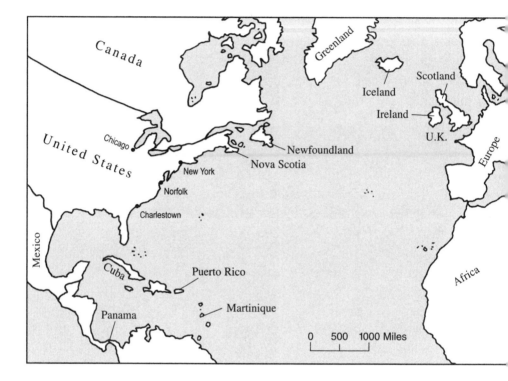

Atlantic Ocean

Chapter 10

A Friendly Invasion – July 1941

Once we were underway, the truth finally leaked out. It was officially confirmed that we were conducting an agreed-upon occupation of Iceland. It proved to be the first overseas deployment of U.S. Marines in a world-wide war that would last almost five years for American forces.

While at sea, we seldom heard the news that affected us. So it was something of a shock to find that we were invading Iceland. The friendly invasion had been announced by President Roosevelt as an executive agreement—a term that was unclear to most Americans. Basically, he just decided we'd move in and the British would move out.

Later, people confused this move with war plans that had been drawn up in the 1930s. Every country that could possibly be invaded by the U.S. was given a color under the Rainbow Plan. Iceland was war-plan Indigo. Call it what you will, all I know is that it did not go well with folks back home. We later learned that Congress disapproved strongly and the Germans were making threats about retaliating.

In effect, we were getting another step closer to our unofficial allies, the British, by replacing them as the military force on Iceland. Before them it was the Danish who protected Greenland and Iceland. The Brits had moved in after Germany invaded Denmark in 1940. Our replacing the British was another clear step toward getting into the war. Cousin Al's words kept ringing in my ears. "Joining early is the smart thing to do."

The convoy's trip to Iceland was not without some excitement. We practiced our shooting by blowing up mines that we found drifting at sea. We even helped in the rescue of survivors from a torpedoed ship. Seven people were spotted in a lifeboat and we brought them aboard. Several of them were nurses. Having women on board changed even the veterans—we were on our best behavior.

Two days later, on July 2, we had another grim introduction to the reality of war as we sighted the floating debris of the HMS Hood. The pride of the British Fleet had been instantaneously sunk on May 24 by the notorious German battleship Bismarck. Reports were confirmed that the Hood went down after being hit by one massive volley. Weeks after the battle, the sea was still littered with items from the Hood. *Our spirits were somber after sailing through the remains of that once-great ship.*

It took us a week to get to Iceland, and we unloaded the Marines on shore using the Higgins boats. I remember the island had snow on the mountains. It was very different from our California landings. Balbo Beach was small and rocky—nothing like the wide open and sandy San Clemente—but we dropped the troops just like in the training exercise.

The Higgins boats (then LCPs) did not yet have ramps, and the familiar sight during the war of Marines charging off the landing craft did not happen in Iceland. Instead, they rolled over the gunwales to disembark. Again, nobody shot at us. But that didn't mean we were welcomed by the locals.

"You mean they were unfriendly?" I asked.

No, I think they were scared. Iceland is a small place, isolated, and the people are all descendants from early Viking settlers. Remember, we weren't tourists. We were the military of yet another country, and it was an occupation. The landing made quite an impression—although friendly, it was an invasion.

Later I found this entry in his journal concerning the events in Iceland:

> July 7th, Reykjavik, Iceland. High mountains. Purple in hue and snow capped. The people as cold and strange as the climate, very confused at our appearance after putting up with the British influence for two years.

When my father resumed his story, he changed the topic with a tried-and-true method. He talked about the weather, or to be exact, the sunlight. *At that time of year the north latitudes are almost always in daylight. It caused most of us to act funny because we rarely got any sleep. The best I can explain is that the clock inside your body operates on one time and the ship on another. After a couple weeks were we glad to head home. We thought we would finally get some well-needed rest, but we were wrong.*

The North Atlantic was solid fog and we were miserable around the clock. We were stuck in a fog bank for days and days. It was cold, damp,

46

and as thick as thick can be. Guys like me, on the deck crew, were on what seemed like constant lookout duty. We double manned our posts and were scared that another ship would run into us.

The worst part was the constant alarms from fog horns and whistles. Every two minutes the ship's whistle would go off. Imagine almost a week of whistles and horns without a break. Everyone was on edge from the fog alarms and dead tired from the lack of sleep. Finally, we broke out of the fog bank and headed for the big Naval base at Norfolk, Virginia.

At that point, it was time for us to gas up the car. We pulled into a truck stop somewhere in southern Georgia to get fuel and stretch our legs. As my father headed toward the cashier, I pondered what had changed between us in the past couple of hours. It struck me hard. He was really talking to me. Although I wasn't saying much, it was a conversation and not a lecture. I wanted it to continue. I could tell by his voice and demeanor that the story of *The Gangster's* adventures was just beginning.

I was anxious to get going again on the road.

A Sailor's Memoir

Chapter 11

Getting Ready for War – July to December 1941

As we returned to the highway I hurried my father back into his story. "It was still July of 1941 when you arrived in Norfolk, right?"

Oh yeah, it was still July. I think we got into Norfolk on the 27ᵗʰ and were back out to sea right away on maneuvers. We spent the better part of the next three months in and out of several East Coast ports practicing our loading, unloading, and runs to the beach. We got very good at doing all the jobs related to getting troops and supplies onto a beachhead.

With that good restart I expected him to keep going, but he paused and went somewhere in time and stayed there for more than a few moments. When he resumed his narrative, he purposely jumped ahead to December. I noted the gap, but since he had just shared a year of his hidden life, I said nothing. I very much wanted him to continue in his comfortable manner, so I did not press for an explanation. It was good that I did not.

Several years later, after we had grown closer, my father filled in those missing months. The wait was worth it. By then I knew him well enough to understand why he moved past some events at the time of our trip north.

Here is what I learned: During August of 1941 my father and his shipmates were able to briefly go home on leave. While visiting, my father ended his relationship with a hometown girl. He thoughtfully noted in his journal that "the Navy had given a new light on things" and decided that although she was sweet, she was not as interesting as he had remembered.

This insight into the worldly sailor my father had become was further advanced by his matter-of-fact mention, very briefly, of his courtship and marriage to his first wife. The war brought them together and would later pull them apart. He kept that experience to himself for a long time. I later pieced events together.

After ending the relationship with the hometown girl, he met a beautiful lady from New Hampshire. She was visiting friends near

Boston when the *Fuller* harbored there. A whirlwind August-to-November romance ended with a wedding on November 23, 1941.

He may have kept mum with me for another reason: That date was also my birthday. Maybe that was why he had always shied away from me on that date.

Also, my father was always a complete gentleman when it came to the ladies. Perhaps he held off telling me about his "war bride" out of respect for my mother. He assumed, correctly, that I had no knowledge of this previous marriage and, since it was not part of our family's history, he avoided telling me about it in 1967.

I found, and still find, his thoughtfulness admirable. Later as an adult, I fully understood his hesitancy to discuss certain topics with me at the time. My exposure to his journal came after my father's death in 1983, and when I read the entries for this period, I am profoundly aware that it depicts a young sailor finding love while engaged in wartime adventures. I wonder how I would have reacted to some of the details if he had shared them more fully during our ride. His letting it pass worked out fine. Both of us might have been embarrassed by his journal:

> Also the fact that I realized I had fallen in love. So much astonished, yet enthused by its forceful reaction, I wanted so much to see Gertrude again... I was walking on air most of the time as Gertrude had me enraptured with herself, so things worked out naturally.

What was unknown to me in 1967, the whirlwind courtship and wedding that saw my father a married man by the beginning of the war, was not crucial to my interest in the story that was unfolding. I was focused on the events of early December 1941 and how they affected *The Gangster.*

I urged him on.

By the winter of 1941, almost everyone believed we were going to enter the war. The question was only when. After repainting the ship and going across the North Atlantic in an allied convoy, we just naturally assumed Germany would be the enemy. At that time our eyes were fixed on the war news coming from Europe and not the Pacific.

On the Fuller *we trained hard and were soon known as a tight ship. A couple days into December we were tapped for a solo cruise to the Caribbean. I'm certain it was because of the Chicago connection so many of us had that made us something special. We really did work well together. I don't know how far our nickname had spread, but our shipboard newspaper was already named* The Gangster. *We were proud of who we were and it showed in everything about us.*

Most of the crew saw the assignment as a luxury cruise because it was a routine delivery run. All we had to do was get some supplies to the Navy's base in Cuba, drop off replacement submarine crews in Panama, and deliver depth charges in San Juan, Puerto Rico. When we left Norfolk, our spirits were very high. Duty was light because the sub crews shared some of the watches, and we were having a great time in the warm sunshine.

We were two days out to sea when the news of the attack on Pearl Harbor was received. Everyone's attitude changed in an instant because we were running alone and carrying explosives. Watches were doubled, and the ship had to be blacked out completely at night. The trip was no longer routine and a new reality sunk in fast. We were at war, and we were extremely vulnerable.

After a few days, Hitler surprised us all and declared war on the United States, so we also had to contend with German U-boats. For two weeks we continued the mission under extreme caution. Our nerves were constantly on edge. For months, German submarine wolf packs had been sinking merchant vessels all along the East Coast, and it is a miracle that we avoided contact with them. We safely made the entire trip alone and were extremely glad when we reached Norfolk. What started for us as a lark ended on a very serious note.

Our Christmas that year was quiet and very somber.

Even ships in dry dock at Pearl Harbor were targets. The destroyer USS *Shaw* took three hits from dive bombers on December 7, 1941.

THE LADY GANGSTER

Chapter 12

War – Early 1942

As one of the defining moments of twentieth century history, the surprise raid on Pearl Harbor pushed America out of isolation and into the world conflict. Two waves of over 350 Japanese aircraft from six carriers struck a devastating blow on that sleepy Sunday morning in Hawaii.

The immediate impact was shocking. The U.S. Navy lost five ships—two of them battleships—188 aircraft, and suffered 2,388 deaths and 1,178 wounded. Fifty-seven civilians were killed. Additionally, six battleships, three cruisers, and one destroyer were damaged and put out of service. The Japanese lost only 29 aircraft, four midget submarines, and 64 men. Luckily, the raid's timing missed the four aircraft carriers which were out at sea.

A second surprise came on December 11th when Germany joined its ally and declared war on the United States.

"What was it really like when the war finally began?" I had seen film clips and old newsreels, but wanted his first-hand view of what immediately followed the Japanese attack on Pearl Harbor.

All the news was bad. Germany controlled Europe, except for the British Isles, and the Japanese seemed to be taking over all of Asia. Each day's news told of another military post or city falling before the Imperial Japanese Army, Navy, and Marines. People were scared. The cities on both U.S. coasts were blacked out at night, and there were practice air-raid alarms both day and night at the bases we visited.

For about a month or so, we ran up and down the coast between North Carolina and New York. I can't remember what we delivered on those trips, but we finally docked in New York for a few days and loaded up with troops and medical personnel sometime in mid-February. Soon we left for Canadian waters and, like before, linked up with more ships to make a run across the North Atlantic. That time we went all the way, as our destination was Belfast, Northern Ireland. Once again, we were on the alert for German submarines that were sinking a good number of ships. On this crossing, there was no doubt that we were a preferred target.

In February 1942, German U-boats were plentiful in the North Atlantic. They sat beyond the protection of air patrols and attacked all the convoys. But they were unable to get near the Fuller *due to the heavy escort that traveled with us. A large number of destroyers and destroyer escorts had been assigned to make certain every member of the First British Expeditionary Force arrived safely. The "cans," as destroyers were known, raced around the convoy constantly, and I remember they seemed to drop a lot of depth charges.* The U-boats were kept at bay and our human cargo was delivered without a *scratch. We quickly unloaded at Belfast and immediately headed for Scotland.*

We raced across the Irish Sea to see if the Fuller *or another transport, the* Neville, *would reach Glasgow first. We won bragging rights after they ran aground. The* Neville's *crew was really embarrassed because one of the worst things for a ship's reputation is to get beached by mistake. It was really hard on them since the "inexcusable" error took place during our race. They took a lot of ribbing from us whenever we saw them on liberty in Glasgow.*

"Were you in Scotland very long?"

Long enough to drink warm beer and Scotch whiskey. He laughed at his memory of visiting the local pubs. *The bottles of beer were stacked on shelves and when you ordered, the barman just reached over and opened one. We were used to cold beers, but you couldn't find any in Scotland. The locals thought we were joking when we asked for cold ones.*

One thing I remember clearly is how poor everyone seemed. The war had taken its toll on all the businesses, and the shops were short on just about everything. The U-boats had cut them off from almost all supplies, and items as basic as food were really hard to find.

However, the general gloom of the weather and short supplies did not seem to affect the Scots very much. We were some of the first Americans to arrive as allies and they were very friendly. They also were more than willing to sell us their best whiskey. Our cash went far in their pubs, and it was during that visit that I developed my appreciation for single malts.

Indeed, my father did not drink very much, but when he did I observed that he seldom touched anything other than good Scotch whiskey. Some lessons learned stay with you all your life, he told me.

It was a short stay and an eye-opening experience. I saw how tough the British people could be. They held out alone against the Nazis and suffered a great deal for almost two years. Although it was pretty far north, Glasgow had experienced air raids and had some bombed-out buildings to show for it. We saw firsthand some of the effects that war had on regular people, and it made us take our duties even more seriously. All of us would have liked to stay longer in Scotland, but the Fuller was a transport, and there was a special cargo for us to move across the ocean.

A Sailor's Memoir

Chapter 13

Refugees and Wolf Packs

The Fuller *could move any type cargo, but our specialty was transporting people. When we sailed into Glasgow we were empty. When we left, we were loaded with an odd bunch of refugees headed for North America.*

At this point I am able to augment my father's account with a quotation from another source. Albert C. Allen, another member of *The Gangster's* crew, served as a signalman, and before leaving the ship at the war's end, penned an account which followed the same chronology as my father's journal and oral history. Allen's account is semi-official in nature, as he had access to the ship's log and action reports. Also, Allen's work is remembered, by some *Fuller* crew members, as having been commissioned and reviewed by the ship's leadership, and perhaps even sanitized at the request of higher-ups. Therefore, in the future it will be referred to as "the ship's account."

This is how that account described the return trip from Scotland:

> We left "bonnie" Scotland on the fourteenth of March, carrying a load of French and Scottish Canadians, and five civilian women who came from God knows where. Our progress through the Irish Sea was enlivened that night by a series of events which are funny only in retrospect. Things started out in confusion, for that evening our force ran through another convoy on the narrow confines of the Irish Sea, and for a good half hour ships heeled way over in tight turns, were backed down, blew whistles, and showed dimmed lights. Why there were no collisions is a question that only the Almighty can answer.

That was an interesting cruise. The French-Canadians had music in their souls, and sang the whole trip away with such little ditties as "Alouetta," to the accompaniment of an accordion. There was also a Scottish Major who daily made a tour of the boat decked in kilts and bag-pipe playing "The Campbells Are Coming."

To top it all off, just as we were about to enter New York harbor we ran into a wolf pack of German subs. The auxiliaries promptly turned around and headed back in the general direction of Scotland, while the escort, aided by blimps from the coastal patrol, held field day on the pig-boats, and we finally wandered in on the 29th, only a day late.

Submarines were often called "pigboats" because the combination of diesel fuel, cigarette smoke, and scores of bodies that went unwashed for months created a powerful aroma in their interiors.

My father recalled that in addition to lying in wait outside New York, the U-boats were a threat throughout the trip. It was not until 1943-44, when air cover was extended through the use of small escort carriers, that the U-boats' domination of shipping lanes was challenged.

From the time we left Scotland, we were on constant watch for periscope wakes and torpedoes. We never sighted either, but the escorts were active like they were on the way over. The excitement did not stop until we docked in New York. You'd be surprised to learn that the subs were the thickest not far from home. The Germans were really bold about getting close to our coast and they would have loved to sink us in the Hudson River.

When we left New York a few days later we again had heavy escorts, even though we were supposed to hug the coast all the way to Norfolk. Some real bad weather knocked us all about and we had to make a run for it alone.

The Fuller *was actually better suited than the escorts for bad conditions. Our hull was longer and quite a bit wider than the average tin can [destroyer]. The cans were faster, but we could take rough seas much better.*

There were many times that The Gangster *out-performed the ships assigned to protect her. Our solo cruise in the Caribbean, and this gale-blown run to Norfolk, were just the first examples of many trips* The Gangster *would complete alone or with a single escort.*

At Norfolk we were put in the yard for some revisions to our gear. Work crews added some cargo booms and thickened our armor plating. We thought nothing of the changes at the time. Little did we suspect that the next trip would take us through the Panama Canal and back into the Pacific Ocean. There we would land troops and be shot at quite often, and the extra armor would be needed.

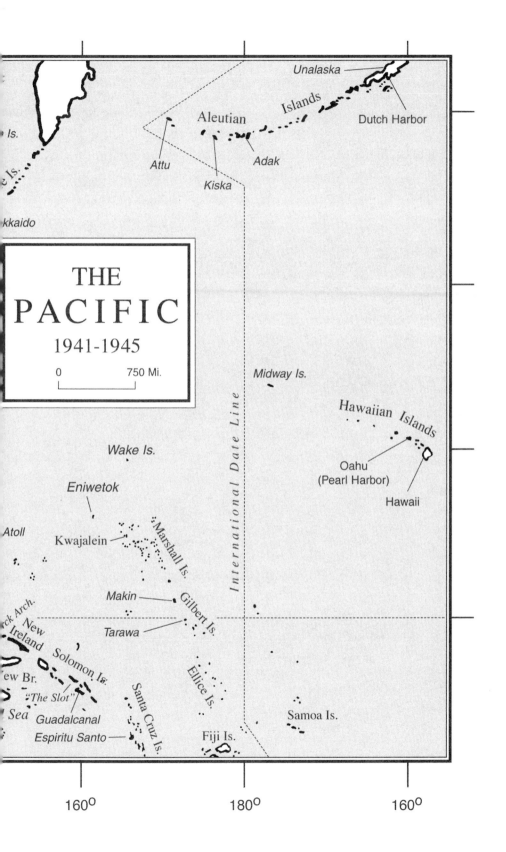

Is.

e Is.

kkaido

Unalaska

Aleutian   Islands

Dutch Harbor

Attu   Adak

Kiska

THE
PACIFIC
1941-1945

0   750 Mi.

Midway Is.

Hawaiian Islands

Wake Is.

Oahu
(Pearl Harbor)

Eniwetok

Hawaii

Atoll

Kwajalein

Marshall Is.

International Date Line

Makin   Gilbert Is.

Tarawa

ck Arch.

New
Ireland   Solomon Is.

Ellice Is.

ew Br.

"The Slot"

Sea   Guadalcanal

Santa Cruz Is.

Samoa Is.

Espiritu Santo

Fiji Is.

160°   180°   160°

A Sailor's Memoir

Chapter 14

Back To the Pacific – April 1942

By this time in my father's story, I was in complete awe of *The Gangster*'s travels and exploits. I knew a fair amount about the war and placed what I had just heard in perspective. At the war's start, America had a small army, and its navy was "on the ropes," reeling from the sneak attack at Pearl Harbor. England was the lone holdout against Germany in Western Europe, and the Russians had yet to begin their recovery from Hitler's march east into their country. In the Pacific, the first six months of the war saw the Japanese military machine conquer territory after territory without meeting serious opposition. My father and the Chicago Boys, by joining early, were an important part of America's effort to turn things around. I wanted to know more and I urged him on.

"How did you end up in the Pacific?" I asked.

It was pretty simple. We were desperately needed there. The Navy was spread really thin. Also, and most important, we could land men on beaches with our Higgins boats, and the Pacific war was going to be fought on beaches.

When the Fuller *was commissioned in 1941, there were less than a dozen ships like her. Her class—Heywood—was named after the first of the passenger/cargo liners converted as transports. At first the* Heywoods *were designated as APs, or just transports. Later, we were re-assigned new numbers as APAs, or attack transports, to reflect our role as the delivery system for assault troops. APAs were always in the thick of things. If the Marines got anywhere first, we got them there.*

We became attack transports because we had the Higgins boats, and knew how to use them. The Fuller *and her sister ships became the backbone of the amphibious force that developed in the first couple years of the war. No attack transports—no invasions.*

When we took those refugees from Glasgow to New York, it was a pier-to-pier delivery. Almost any transport could have done that. Heck, they even converted luxury liners like the Queen Mary *for that kind of duty. Hauling troops from one port to another is passenger duty.*

The Fuller *and her sister ships were special. The Pacific Fleet needed to put fighting men on beaches. In the end, it was real simple as to why we went back to the Pacific. A job needed doing and we were the ones to do it. We had the equipment and training that fit the job.*

I just wish there had been more of us. We left Norfolk and didn't come home for a long time.

That's when a true love for history hit me. I had always been interested in history, but my father's matter-of-fact explanation of events made the details of history—the facts, dates, the places and names—come alive and make sense in a real-life manner. I was more than hooked on the story of his adventure. I knew then that there was truth and real meaning in what had previously been presented to me in school as boring lists of data. For me, the key to history would forever be the intertwining of information with an interesting personal tale.

Here is more from the ship's account which indeed reads more like a log entry:

> On April the tenth we left Norfolk with two other transport divisions, escorted by ten destroyers, a cruiser and the battleship *Texas*. We dropped the escort at Balboa and proceeded through the Canal. On the other side, we were dismayed to find our escort weak, to say the least. (Weak, that is, in comparison to what we were accustomed to on the East Coast.) There were six destroyers and two of the old 7,500 ton cruisers. In company with these, and for about 25 miles, a squadron of PT boats, we left the Panama coast and headed out across the Pacific.

The ship's account ended with the same sad comment of my father's recounting:

It was more than two years before we would
return to the United States.

As I previously mentioned, there was a year-long gap in my father's journal. When it resumed at about this time in the story of the *Fuller* he prefaced it with an insightful comment:

Time has added to our experiences and all of us are "Salts"
now.

The prophetic comment of the old chief petty officer had come true. The sea had made sailors out of the Midwestern city residents who, less than two years earlier, had never seen a ship. In the spring of 1942, the Chicago Boys, traveling on their *Gangster*, were an important asset of the U.S. Navy as they headed into the Pacific.

The ship's account describes how the *Fuller* began the next portion of its adventures:

The trip across the Pacific was quiet and
peaceful. A day out of Pago Pago, the task
unit split up; our division to proceed to
Samoa, while the others were to go to the
Fiji Islands. Our division rendezvoused
with the cruiser, *Honolulu*, and two
destroyers within an hour after leaving the
others, and continued on to our destination. Unloading our troops and cargo at
Pago Pago and at Apia without incident, we
proceeded to Wellington, New Zealand,
arriving there on May 22nd.

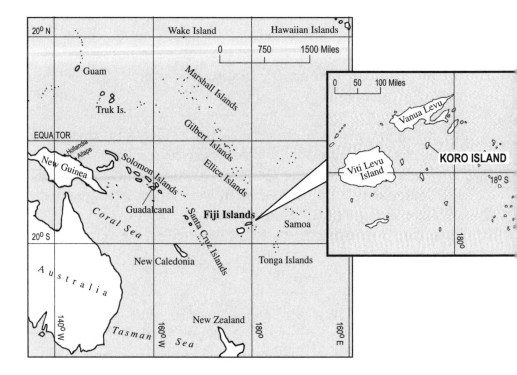

Southwest Pacific

Chapter 15

Heaven is Named New Zealand – May 1942

Whenever my father spoke about New Zealand, his entire demeanor changed. I never saw him more calm and relaxed. Just the mention of New Zealand would send him to a place in time and memory that was forever a bit of heaven for him.

He picked up his story in May 1942 when the *Fuller* arrived at Wellington. *When we got to New Zealand, we might as well have been saints entering heaven. The people loved us. And, I'm not exaggerating at all. They really loved us and they showed it in every possible way.*

As part of the British Empire, the New Zealanders were very loyal to England and jumped into the war in 1939. Most of their military-aged men had been gone for three years or more. When we arrived at the dock in Wellington, we were surprised to see only boys and old men in the crowds. The folks who met us were very happy to see young men of fighting age. The Japanese were not that far away, and we were the first Americans to "come to the rescue" so to speak.

The semi-official ship's account of Kiwi-American relations is:

Now, since May 1942, "Wellington" has for us been a synonym for "Heaven." Our squadron was apparently the first U.S. ships to visit that port since the beginning of the war, and the gratitude of the New Zealanders was added to their natural friendliness, producing a welcome unequalled anywhere. On our part, Wellington was the first evidence of civilization we had seen in the Pacific, and the ship's company responded wholeheartedly to the welcome of the people. The natural result was a bond between them which grew steadily day by day. A number of marriages occurred between

sailors and the New Zealand girls, as well
as innumerable friendships, platonic and
otherwise, which still endure.

Friendships of the "otherwise" variety were indeed numerous and no doubt interesting. My father explained how easily they were established. *The local girls, as well as their families, were starving for the company of young men. As we stepped off the gangway of the ship we were met by complete strangers who literally grabbed us and took us to their homes. They fed, entertained, and toured us as if we were long-lost family. I can't tell you how great it was to eat home-cooked food and sleep in a real bed. Imagine: We were on the other side of the world preparing for the fight of our lives and we were fortunate beyond belief. I have nothing but good things to say about New Zealand and its wonderful people.*

At the time I first heard about this portion of the *Fuller's* travels, my young imagination produced scenes fit for a B-grade war movie full of romances, tearful departures, and broken hearts. Over the years, as our relationship grew, my father replaced my imagined events with numerous descriptions of New Zealand's small towns, sheep farms, and hardworking citizens. The people he described seemed amazingly similar to those I knew as I grew up in the Midwest. If he was involved with a "local girl" he, true to form, never said anything that could be inferred as confirmation. In addition to the tales about the warm welcome, he did describe several shipyard incidents that were his version of "Yankee Ingenuity Meets the British Commonwealth."

Here are two of his favorites: *One day we were in the dry dock scraping and preparing the* Fuller's *bottom for painting. We were under the loose supervision of the local shipyard workers at the time.*

An older boss told us to carefully mark the waterline for painting, and I hesitated in ordering my work detail to follow his orders. He noticed my foot dragging over his instructions and asked me why. I explained that his way was slower than what I had in mind. He was upset, of course, and told me to show him how his way was wrong. My solution only took some string and chalk.

I had our work detail chalk up a string long enough to stretch the full length of the ship. I told them to hold it in place on both ends of the ship at the top of where the water line should be. Then, I just plucked the string. It hit the hull and left a perfect line for the top of where we would paint. Then I had them drop it a couple of feet and we repeated the move. After that we did the same thing on the other side of the ship. In less than an hour we had painted the space between the lines on both sides. The dockyard workers had never seen anything like it and stood shaking their heads at "those clever Yanks."

We were always interested in cutting corners on work details because we couldn't wait to go on liberty. It was not long after the waterline job that we got assigned the larger task of re-painting the entire deck of the Fuller. The locals were again amused at our labor-saving approach to any kind of work.

After computing the amount of paint we would need for the job, we stationed paint cans at key points across the deck. First, we carefully did the trim work that required attention to edges and corners. Then we did the wide expansion of the deck. The deck areas normally took the most time—it was the biggest part of the job. But, in this case, we sped through the effort by using brand new cut-off mops as large paint brushes. With the edges trimmed, painting was as easy as swabbing the deck. We finished in record time and were on liberty very early that day.

Although some of the *Fuller's* dockyard work methods may have amused the News Zealanders, they were serious preparations for an important operation. On July 22nd, after two glorious months in Wellington, the *Fuller* and other transports loaded elements of the 1st Marines and departed in the company of heavy escort. Five cruisers— USS *Chicago*, USS *Salt Lake City*, HMAS *Australia*, HMAS *Hobart*, and HMAS *Canberra*—joined with a squadron of destroyers as protection for the group as it headed to the Fijis. Three more cruisers and another transport squadron were met off Koro Island and a much larger task force, designated as Number 62, then assembled to prepare for an amphibious landing in the Solomons.

The coral reefs of Koro Island were found wanting as a place to unload troops, but a week of practice landings was conducted nonetheless. Operation Watchtower continued to move forward, and although the Marines would call it Operation Shoestring, in the end a total of seventy-six ships and 635 aircraft would convene off Guadalcanal to conduct the first U.S. amphibious landing on a hostile shore.

Vice Admiral Ghormley reminded all participants that the endeavor was indeed serious. Word from his headquarters was sent out: "We look to you to electrify the world with news of a real offensive. Allied ships, planes and fighting men carry on from Midway. Sock 'em in the Solomons."

Chapter 16

Landing on Guadalcanal – August 1942

In 1939, the renowned military analyst, B.H. Liddell Hart, had written: "A landing on a foreign coast in the face of hostile troops has always been one of the most difficult operations of war. It has now become almost impossible because of the vulnerable target which a convoy of transports offers to the defender's air force as it approaches shore. Even more vulnerable to air attack is the process of disembarkation in open boats."

On the morning of August 7, 1942, the *Fuller* was one of the first ships to conduct the amphibious landing that would begin the well-known island-hopping trek of the Pacific War. Guadalcanal was one of the longest and hardest fought battles of that war and would become famous for many reasons. It was the first major offensive action against the Japanese, and Guadalcanal was the crucial point to halt the Japanese advance which was about to isolate Australia.

The six-month-long battle was closely watched on the home front. Henderson Field, Cactus Air Force, Tokyo Express, The Slot, Iron-Bottom Sound,and Bloody Ridge are a few of the names made famous by Guadalcanal. During the campaign, five major sea battles and three major land battles were fought. Daily air battles and fierce combat on shore caused heavy losses for both sides. Of an estimated 36,000 Japanese defenders, approximately 25,000 died.

The Allies committed a total of 60,000 troops to the campaign. The Marines sustained 1,207 dead, and the Army lost 562. Additionally, 420 airmen and 4,911 seamen were killed. The Allies lost twenty-nine ships and 615 aircraft. Winning did not come cheap, but Guadalcanal was where the Allied forces stopped the Japanese advance. About Guadalcanal, Admiral William F. "Bull" Halsey, Jr. said, "Before Guadalcanal the enemy advanced at his pleasure—after Guadalcanal he retreated at ours." Until our auto trip, I had no idea my father was there.

I listened intently when my father calmly stated that the *Fuller* landed the first troops on Guadalcanal, and I was filled with pride. I nearly burst when he nonchalantly added that the LCP he commanded placed the very first Marine on shore. The skills he had successfully learned in the San Diego surf had earned him the right to skipper the *Fuller's* number one Higgins boat.

My father's claim was corroborated by Donald Langer, a member of the 1st Marine Division, in his account of landing on Guadalcanal from the *Fuller*. "[I] sailed to Fiji (and Guadalcanal) aboard USS *Fuller*, I landed on Guadalcanal in the second Higgins Boat to go ashore, no opposition."

I was very silent as my father spoke about the landings and what happened afterward.

The fight for Guadalcanal began almost two years to the day after I joined the Navy. At the time we put the first Marines ashore, I remembered thinking about that fact. We were lucky that day. I don't think the enemy had any idea we were coming.

There was very little action on Guadalcanal, but nearby on the small island of Tulagi it was different. The Japanese were real thick over there and dug in good. We could faintly hear the sounds of the fighting as we unloaded Marines on Guadalcanal. The opposing troops on Guadalcanal were mostly construction types—working on the airfield. It wasn't until some time later that the Japanese reinforced them and put up a fight. That fight would last for months.

The land battles on Guadalcanal get a great deal of notice, as they should. But the Navy was also hard pressed there. We lost a lot of ships near Guadalcanal. Two of them, the Wasp *and the* Hornet, *were carriers.*

Like I said, at first it was easy. We worked all that first day and kept unloading through the night. The next day was when the planes started coming.

On August 7, 1942, elements of the 1st Marine Division land on Guadalcanal. Observe that the Higgins boats are the older version (LCPs) without front ramps.

The following account is from the *Fuller's* Action Report for August 8th with the first sighting of Japanese planes:

> At 1158 heavy firing was heard from the northeasterly direction and at 1202 planes were observed coming around the eastern end of Florida Island. These planes were flying close to the water, altitude about 100 feet. They appeared to be flying in sections of three in a loose "Vee" and the total number was estimated at twenty. The plane formation split up; approximately half of it heading for the area in which our squadron was operating. Two sections of

four and three planes respectively crossed the bow of the *McCawley* (Task Force 62's flagship) and headed directly for this ship. On nearer approach five of these planes turned right and took a converging course, and two of them swung to the left and passed astern. These planes were taken under fire by the starboard 3" battery as soon as they came in range. The 20mm battery, group 1 and 3, opened fire when the range had closed to approximately 1,500 yards.

One plane passing astern turned right as it approached and came within 200 yards of the stern, apparently intent on strafing the ship. This plane was under fire of group 3 and the 20mm battery at point-blank range. Tracers were entering the nose of the plane and the gunners were raking the fuselage systematically. This plane rolled over and crashed just off the port quarter. The second plane which had also been under fire by both 3" and 20mm batteries swung to the left and crashed beyond the *George F. Elliott*. This was not the plane which later crashed aboard that vessel.

The planes proceeding up the starboard side were being engaged by group 3 of the 3" battery and group 1 of the 20mm battery. Tracers from the 20mm guns could be seen entering the planes and the damage inflicted was plainly visible. When about 600-800 yards from the ship, the leading plane exploded in flames. The conflagration extended about 200 yards and temporarily shut off the view of the remaining planes. The leading plane of the four remaining came in close on the starboard bow then banked right to a course approximately parallel to that of the ship. It continued forward followed by fire from gun #1, and from gun #2 which opened fire as soon as the target's advance permitted that gun to bear. The plane was encased in shrapnel bursts and finally went down well forward. The three remaining planes passed close ahead and were taken under fire by gun #1 as it bore by group 2 of the 20mm battery as they crossed the bow. The port motor of the leading plane of this group was set afire by group 2 of the 20mm battery and fire into the fuselage was continued until the plane crashed in flames on the port bow. The remaining two planes were already burning and severely damaged as a result of the fire in succession by group 2 of the 20mm battery as they crossed ahead and both crashed on the port bow.

While the engagement was going on to the starboard, #4 gun engaged a plane on the port beam outside the formation. Fire was continued on this plane until it exploded in the air. It is probable that this plane was also under fire from other ships.

In its first engagement, *The Gangster* lived up to its name and image. The boys from Chicago accounted themselves well and fended off the aerial attack. However, it did not go as well for the USS *Elliott* which caught fire and had to be abandoned after another plane crashed onto its deck.

The tempo of action had quickened with that day's air attack. And soon, the news of an approaching Japanese naval task force prompted a controversial decision that would mar Navy-Marine Corps relations for some time.

Navy leadership authorized a withdrawal of support forces from Guadalcanal prior to completion of their mission. The Navy was pulling out the transports, even though 1,400 Marines and half the division's supplies were still on board. For the approximately 17,000 Marines on shore, supplies were short. They were left with only seventeen days of food rations and four days of all types of ammunition. Even with captured supplies, the meals for the next six weeks were meager and never more than two a day. To further complicate matters, the 2nd Marine Division headquarters element had not landed.

The Navy's decision may have been a sound one, since the defenseless transports were savory targets for the fast-approaching Japanese. Also at that time, no one knew the coming night's Battle of Savo Island would see four Allied cruisers sunk. So many ships met their end in that locale that it became known as "Iron Bottom Sound."

For the *Fuller* and her sister transports, the night was extremely tense. The ships spent the hours of darkness moving at sea and playing "cat and mouse." They were the prize which had brought the Japanese Imperial Navy into the area, and they had to stay one step ahead although they were not able to go far. The *Fuller's* captain eased his ship into a squall formation and moved about all night under the cover of almost constant rain.

It was a miracle that the *Fuller* and the others were not sunk. The Japanese naval commander (Mikawa) did not capitalize on his tremendous success at Savo Island just north of Guadalcanal, and retreated after sinking the cruisers *Quincy*, *Vincennes*, *Astoria,* and *Canberra* and heavily damaging the cruiser *Chicago*. The Battle of Savo Island was one of the most one-sided defeats suffered in American Naval history.

My father told me how they helped rescue survivors from the battle.

Over a thousand Allied sailors were killed that night and almost as many were wounded and drifting in open waters. We spent the next day pulling them out of oil slicks and away from circling sharks. Most were from the Aussie cruiser Canberra. *It was especially difficult bringing the dead on board.*

From the ship's account:

> We were ordered to take on survivors of the *Canberra*, and the destroyers, *Patterson* and *Blue*, came alongside with their pitiful cargo. The Australians, for the most part, had only what they were wearing, if anything, and were most grateful when the *Fuller's* ship's company opened their lockers to them and provided all possible assistance.
>
> We retired from the Guadalcanal area on August 9th, and happy as we were to be leaving the area, our happiness was spiked with sadness, for the remainder of the cruise to Noumea, the casualty lists of the four cruisers mounted daily, and the burials were held twice. We arrived at Noumea on the 13th, and transferred the remainder of the *Canberra* survivors to the hospital there.

Donald Lutes, another original Chicago Boy, had transferred from the deck to become a Pharmacist's Mate in 1942. As part of the *Fuller's* medical staff he treated the *Canberra's* survivors and confirmed that "three or four *Canberra* crew died aboard the *Fuller*."

My father recounted this portion of his story only once: *We placed the dead sailors in bags, the kind used as covers for mattresses. Weights were also put in the bags, at their feet. Scrap metal was used. We made certain that they had decent clothes on and then sewed the bags shut. There was a ceremony led by our chaplain and we sang some hymns. Then they were slid into the ocean. No grave, no markers. That's how you go at sea. Somebody at home gets a letter, nothing else.*

One member of the *Canberra's* crew, A.V. Fellors, gratefully included a tribute to the rescuers in his poem, "Tulagi," named for the small nearby island north of Guadalcanal. The final stanzas read:

> Late at night, action sounded,
> In the *Canberra's* side projectiles pounded,
> And to their guns the sailors bounded,
> To help save Tulagi.

> The men were almost in their stride,
> When a Japanese torpedo hit our side,
> Causing some brave lads to reel and die,
> Saving Tulagi.

> Although we could not help the fleet,
> Our wounded Captain kept his feet,
> He was one who didn't admit defeat,
> When we sank at Tulagi.

> We are proud of the *Patterson*, and the *Blue*,
> The USS *Fuller* and their sailors too,
> When they braved the shells to save our crew,
> Off the island of Tulagi.

The *Canberra* lost 82 men, including her captain.

The defeat at "Iron Bottom Sound" had decimated the transports' covering force, and withdrawal was a prudent move. Although the Allied naval force collected survivors and removed them to safety, the Marines saw it as "cut and run." Those troops left on the Guadalcanal considered the Navy's departure as an act bordering on cowardice.

Retreat added to the perception that only incompetence could have caused the colossal defeat, and casualties mounted in other ways. Captain Riefkohl of the *Vincennes*, commander of a portion of the Allied forces, lived on as a broken man after losing his ship. Captain Bode of the *Chicago*, also in partial command that night, killed himself.

The defeat (and shame ?) was Navy-wide. The Battle of Savo Island was kept secret for two months and its details were not shared until the relative victory of Allied naval forces at Cape Esperance could be told.

My father was not very charitable when he described the day after the Battle of Savo Island. *I'm not saying we ran with our tail between our legs, but it did hang low. The Navy didn't waste any time hanging around the waters near Guadalcanal. But the boys on the* Fuller *were proud that we came back (to Guadalcanal) as fast as possible and we kept coming. We weren't scared of nothin'.*

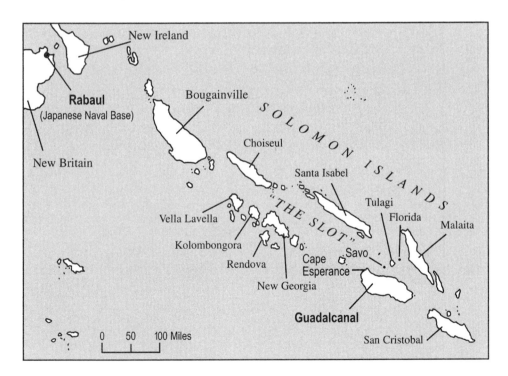

The Solomons and Guadalcanal

Elements of the Marine 2nd Raider Batallion land on Guadalcanal from the "old style" Higgins boats.

Chapter 17

Sprinting In and Out of "The Canal"

When the Marines on Guadalcanal were left on August 8, 1942, to their own resources and short on supplies, the unpleasant talk soon began. At times descriptions of the Navy's retreat reached an almost legendary level of abandonment. One Marine's account, accurate or not, clearly lays out the dismay felt by the troops: "Everybody hauled ass and never came back."

One exception in the accounts told by Guadalcanal Marines would be *The Gangster.*

During the first months of the fighting on Guadalcanal it seemed like we were in and out of there every other day, my father explained. *The guys on the beach were always happy to see us. Once, on a run to the beach in my Higgins boat, a Marine declared, "That must be the only ship left in the Navy!" They really got used to the* Fuller *being around and always were friendly with us.*

More than thirty years later, I witnessed the high regard the Marines had for the *Fuller* when I attend my first reunion of Guadalcanal veterans. There was no inter-service rivalry. Grateful Marines pummeled me with their personal accounts of elation at seeing "that beautiful ship."

From the ship's account, August 13, 1942:

A division of transports, including the *Fuller*, proceeded to Wellington, where we reloaded in five days and returned to our base at Noumea. From there we proceeded to Espiritu Santo, and thence again to Guadalcanal.

From that time, there began a series of runs with Guadalcanal as one end of the run, and the other varying between Noumea

and Santo. This period is distinguished
only by its constant strain of air raids,
the dodging of Jap surface forces which
were never far distant, the speedy unload-
ings, and the retirements. During this
time, the *Fuller* frequently lifted loads of
troops and cargo from other transports at
advance bases and made the run to
Guadalcanal in their places.

The accounts by Marines on Guadalcanal often leave the impression that they were alone for as much as thirty days following the initial landing. However, the *Fuller* was back, as reported, delivering much needed supplies and replacements within days. One eyewitness account has the *Fuller* in Tulagi's harbor on September 1, 1942, helping set up a seaplane re-fueling spot. It took place well within the period that caused ill will between the Navy and Marines.

My father told me more about this time: *We were quick. The* Fuller *ran faster than other transports. We hit 20 knots at times. Boy, that old girl could move, but she'd shake as she did her absolute top speed. And our crew could load and unload fast, too. By then we had been together for two years and we really made things hum.*

Elgin Bowen, another of the Chicago Boys, described *The Gangster* during this time: *We were a good ship, a lucky ship, a happy ship.*

An unidentified series of entries in a journal found in my father's papers describes the supply runs, the air raids, and the threat from Japanese surface forces.

> September 3 – 0830 Sailed Noumea with AK [Attack Cargo]
> *Bellatrix* and 3 APDs [Troop Transport-High
> Speed].
> September 5 – 0630 Arrived Espiritu Santo, New Hebrides.
> September 6 – Sailed Espiritu Santo with AK *Bellatrix*, 4
> APDs and 1DD [Destroyer].
> September 8 – Arrived Guadalcanal, Solomon Islands. 1600
> Pulled anchor and steamed to Tulagi Harbor

19 miles away. 1930, 2 bombers attacked at bridge height, their bombs missing by 35 yds. The planes had their running lights on and we thought the planes friendly until bombs fell.

2000 Sailed when observation plane reported a Jap cruiser and 10 DDs coming in for us. 3 hrs. later the Jap fleet came in, searched for us with their lights, sank a YP Boat [Training Craft] and shelled the beach. We cruised that night in the Indispensable Straits.

September 9 – 1130 attacked by high level bombers just off Lunga Point. The planes laid a perfect pattern around AK *Bellatrix*, but no direct hits. 1 Jap bomber and 2 U.S. fighters hit the water. 1534 Dropped anchor at Tulagi. 1730 Sailed with *Bellatrix*, 5 APDs.

September 11 – 1630 Arrived Espiritu Santo, New Hebrides.

September 12 - 1300 Sailed Espiritu Santo with *Bellatrix* and 1DD.

September 13 – 1630 2nd DD joined convoy.

September 14 – 0810 Arrived Tulagi, Solomon Islands. 0957 Air raids, cruised until 1118. 1330 Air raid, cruised until 1500. 1757 Air raid. Sailed, leaving behind our boats, boat crews, and 2 officers who were ashore when the raid began. A DD downed 2 of attacking planes, could see sky lit up by fires caused by bombers at Guadalcanal.

September 15 – 1 DD left to join task force at 0800. 0900 4 Jap bombers sighted us.

One marine, Dana T. Hughes of the Third Barrage Balloon Squadron, recalls how the Marines viewed *The Gangster* during this period. In his memoirs, he writes: "By mid-morning on Tuesday 15 September 1942, things suddenly changed! Like an old-time sailor spotting land after a long ocean cruise, someone up on Tulagi's Government Hill shouted, 'there's a ship approaching from the 'Canal.' Moments later, looking closer, we could see two ships coming into sight: A can and an AKA [AP]... And they were still heading toward Tulagi. God! At long last, our Savior: The USS *Fuller*. Sure enough, she rounded the point, eased into Tulagi Harbor, and dropped anchor about one hundred yards off the Government Wharf, where most of my squadron had by now gathered, and were cheering a lusty welcome."

During this period the *Fuller* clearly became the "go to" ship for resupply of the Marines on Guadalcanal. In setting the standard for quick in–and–out unloading under difficult and dangerous circumstances, *The Gangster* earned her skipper, Captain Theiss, a significant honor.

The ship's account is matter of fact in its description:

```
It was for this period that Captain
Theiss received the Navy Cross for safely
conducting a task unit through a particu-
larly deadly series of air attacks, safely
unloading cargo, and retiring from the area
with no casualties.
```

Receiving the Navy's second-highest decoration was no small feat. The awarding of the Navy Cross did not happen just because some supplies were delivered. The *Fuller*, through its Captain, was being singled out for exemplary service. Additionally, the *Fuller* would pay a price for the recognition and lose her talented Captain to a reassignment that can only be seen as another honor for the ship, as well as the man.

Captain Theiss was soon to become Chief of Staff to Admiral R.K. Turner, then Commander of Amphibious Force, South Pacific, and later to become Commander, Amphibious Forces, U.S. Pacific Fleet. Theiss was later promoted to the war-time one-star rank of Commodore. It cannot be specifically verified, but it is certainly most probable, that *The Gangster's* later special assignments during the invasions of Saipan,

Tinian, and Okinawa were due to Captain Theiss's firsthand experience with the well-oiled Chicago-based crew.

Good fortune accompanied *The Gangster* and her crew for several more months. But fatigue and the fog of battle finally caught up with them in early November. It was then she sustained her first blow, at friendly hands—her own.

A Sailor's Memoir

Chapter 18

Running Into Friends

There was quite an air war over Guadalcanal. We were very lucky not to have been hit by at least one of those Jap planes. They were always over us, but the Fuller *didn't get a scratch until we did it to ourselves.*

Dad's journal is brief in its description of the collision that put the first scars on *The Gangster*:

> November 2 – 0400 Anchored Guadalcanal. 0900 Air raid –
> cruised until 1100.
> 1932 Rammed DD *Conyngham* amidships.
> Knocked hole in our bow and flooded fire-
> room of DD.
> The *Conyngham* was trying to cross our bow
> to attack task force.
> Coming in to protect us from oncoming Jap
> task force.

The ship's account covered the incident with a few more words:

On that day, we were, as usual, in Guadalcanal unloading cargo when we received a warning that a formation of Japanese destroyers were moving down the "slot."

We completed unloading, as did the ships in company with us; and as dusk set in, retired through Lengo Channel. It was a foul night, with visibility about zero, and the rain pelting like shrapnel. Suddenly the destroyer *Conyngham*, one of our screen, was observed through the rain to be crossing our bow. In maneuvering to avoid another force which was approaching us she had sustained

a steering casualty which jammed her rudder
hard right. There was no time for her to
warn us, and the visibility being what it
was, no chance of seeing anything beyond
five hundred yards. We blew the whistle, and
backed down full, but it was too late. We
hit her just abaft the bridge, knocked off
her forward stack, and flooded her number
one fireroom. Our bow was peeled back from
the stem for about twenty feet and from the
waterline to the keel.

My father was on deck soon after the collision occurred. He
recalled, *I heard an awful grinding and scraping sound. It seemed to come
right up out of the ship's insides. And, if the collision was not enough, the
next moments were very scary. We were almost sunk by some more of our
ships coming to help the damaged destroyer.*

The scene indeed grew crowded as "help" arrived. From the ship's
account:

Suddenly a ship was sighted on the port bow.
We challenged it, and with knees quivering
awaited the reply. We had not long to wait.
It was correct. We learned later that the
formation we so blithely challenged was composed of four cruisers and five "cans", and
that they were virtually certain that we
were the Jap formation and were ready to
open fire when our signal came over.

Another version comes from John B. Beck, CRM, of the *Fuller*: "...so
here is 'the rest of the story.' We (everyone afloat in the South Pacific)
knew that a large convoy of Japs was on their way to Guadalcanal. Task
Force #75 got a fix via radar and sonar on our ships and thought we
were the Jap force, and had their heavy guns trained on us ready to do

battle. However...once again the hand of God...one of the heavy cruisers was straight in line with the *Conynham's* signal gun and were able to read, 'Taking some water in No. 1 Engine room etc.' and decided we were not the Japanese force and moved on.... We never knew they were there. Some few days later at Espirito Santo we saw the remnants of those cruisers after their 'successful' battle that night. I was their Charley [enemy]!"

John Carroll aboard the *Conyngham* had a firsthand view of the damage and a "working sailor's view" of callous Navy Brass. From his account:

> As a member of the damage control party we immediately went down to the #2 fire room where water was pouring through a big hole just above the waterline aft the bulkhead separating the #1 and #2 fire rooms. We worked all night shoring up the hole and was successful enough to hold our own with the water. We were about six inches from shutting down the boilers in #2 fire room. We could only make about five knots to some small islands and we layed [sic] low for a short time. Eventually making our way back and tied up along side the USS *Curtis*, an airplane tender where her chicken-shit admiral would not even give us help of any kind with all the facilities he had aboard. We had not electrical welding at that time aboard so we were helpless putting a plate over the hole. To top it off he barred us from going aboard the *Curtis* and even refused us a ration of bread since we were out. A sea-going tug finally pulled alongside and with their welding gear we were able to put a temporary plate over the hole. We finally made it back to Pearl Harbor for repairs.

The Gangster (and her target) were lucky on several counts. Neither she nor the damaged escort was in danger of sinking from the effects of the collision. Remarkably, a heavy rain squall had cleared the decks of sleeping crew members on the destroyer only minutes before the collision. And, importantly, the proper signal was sent and recognized before a sizeable friendly task force turned unfriendly.

"So how long did that put you out of action?" I asked. By now it was night. I was still driving, wide awake, and totally absorbed by my father's story.

There was a silver lining in the rain clouds that night. We limped all the way back to Wellington and had more than two full months away from Guadalcanal. I thought New Zealand was wonderful our first time there, but the second long stay was even better. We celebrated Thanksgiving, Christmas, and New Year in New Zealand and it was something to remember.

Again, he was short on some of the details.

Chapter 19

Pearl and the Milk Run

He had that look again, so I continued to drive and waited for the story to resume. When it did, the Chicago Boys and *The Gangster* were back on "the milk run," as they called their Guadalcanal supply duty. Once Guadalcanal was totally subdued, it became a vital staging area for the Solomons and a regular destination for the *Fuller.* My father told me about their day-in and day-out grind, and I could not imagine how they could get accustomed to air raids and being chased by Japanese subs, but they did.

Soon we were back on our old route. We could do it in our sleep. We could even spot familiar palm trees on the beaches. He laughed. *If we had thought more about it, we probably could have given names to them.*

From the ship's account:

> There followed a quiet interval of runs between Guadalcanal and the Fiji Islands, punctuated by the daily Japanese air attacks at Guadalcanal, which occurred promptly at ten in the morning and did little damage except to the blood pressure.
>
> From then until October we were back on the old Guadalcanal run, which by this time had taken on all the aspects of a Sunday School outing.

From an account in a second journal among my father's papers there appeared to be at least one unauthorized side trip with some of the Marines the *Fuller* had been supplying. From the entry on February 28, 1943:

0600 Arrived Guadalcanal. Toured island in a Jeep while I was supposed to expedite unloading ashore. Arrived back at ship one-and-half hours after ship was unloaded and had to climb up rope onto fantail. 1700 Underway. Anchored for night in Tulagi Harbor. No air raids that night.

The day-in and day-out routine of supplying Guadalcanal continued until October with one very notable exception. Rumors began to circulate that a trip home was in the works. It made sense. *The Fuller* had been at sea for over a year and a return stateside seemed plausible.

I told you about the scuttlebutt, right?

I nodded.

He went on. *It was going all over the ship and everyone was certain— I mean 100% certain—we were going home. And that's another example of how wrong you could be.*

We went to Pearl Harbor, picked up some more Marines, and returned by way of Australia. We were back on the same old route before we knew it. We were never meant to go home. We were headed for Pearl all along. All we had to show from all that scuttlebutt was disappointment.

However, the disappointment produced a side effect. The crew rebelled, sort of, and my father loved to recount it because the event greatly affected his ship-board duties. The following is what I recall concerning the event that prompted his assignment as the ship's Master at Arms, or better known as "the ship's policeman."

The Navy has some peculiar informal rituals. One of them is the mock pirate take-over of a vessel when crew members traverse the equator for their first time. The crew dons pirate clothes, as best they can re-create, and applies paint to their faces and so on. Marauding bands then "capture" the initiates who are paddled and subjected to various forms of hazing. My father had experienced the ritual with his shipmates the first time they as a crew passed over the equator.

On the trip to Pearl Harbor the news of not going home had hit, and the disgruntled crew got carried away during the equator-crossing ceremonies. My father was somehow scooped up with the rookies and received some misdirected abuse for a second time. He took it in stride although he was well within his rights to complain. His positive attitude was observed by the Captain who saw an advantage in arranging a reassignment of duties for my father.

Soon thereafter, my father, the new Master at Arms, was someone with a clear "bone to pick" with the malcontents who had stepped over the unwritten bounds of shipboard protocol. At least that is how my father always saw it.

He explained it to me. *After my reassignment, the over-exuberant pirates were always on their best behavior. They were looking over their shoulders to see if I was going to retaliate. I think I was always fair and I never knowingly took it out on anyone for my second initiation for crossing the equator. I do know that because of it I was on deck and safe the day we were bombed.*

Crossing the equator and paying homage to King Neptune was an important event for the "pirates" who crewed the *Fuller*. A non-voluntary second turn in this ritual led to a crucial reassignment for my father. He was certain the incident started a chain of events that saved his life.

It was "hands off" for the officers who were only allowed to be spectators at the ritual.

For the enlisted crew members not involved in the "proceedings," the ritual at the equator was great entertainment.

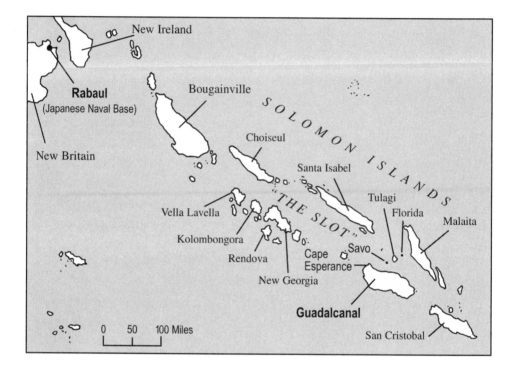

The Solomons and Guadalcanal

Chapter 20

The Day the Bombs Dropped – November 8, 1943

Bougainville was the largest of the Solomon Islands and had been a Japanese stronghold for quite some time. Their retreat from Guadalcanal in early 1943 made it all the more important to hold. If they lost the fight for Bougainville, the Japanese would lose their base at Rabaul and be forced to retreat 800 miles north to Truk. They knew that Bougainville would be assaulted and they were prepared to defend it. The Japanese air attacks were intense.

The Fuller *landed troops on the day after Halloween. I remember how warm it was and not at all like the first of November back home. The surf was rough on the Higgins boats. In that landing some were damaged and even a few were swamped. But, we got all our Marines to the beach safely. We came back a second time with more troops. On that next trip we got hit.*

"You were bombed? From one of those raids? When did the ship get hit?

Yes, we certainly got bombed. It was on our second trip into Bougainville. I was up top. My new Master at Arms duties saved me—I'm sure of that. I would have been in the aft hold at the time if I had not been re-assigned. It's like I said—my new job saved me.

From the ship's account:

> We left Fila on the 28th, passed Guadalcanal to the northward, and headed into the "slot." On the morning of November 1, we put troops ashore on Empress Augusta Bay, Bougainville, in the teeth of heavy mortar and machine gun fire, and to the tune of a pre-invasion shelling by the guns of our escorting destroyers, and the transports' three inch and five inch batteries. The Japs tried an ineffectual air attack that afternoon, but they did not get past the

screen, which proved to everyone's satisfaction that the long gunnery drills had not been wasted. We retired that evening, and returned to Guadalcanal.

But not for long. We spent two days in Tulagi, and again got underway for Bougainville. This was designated as the third echelon and was composed of one transport division under the command of the division commander in the *President Jackson*. We were supposed to be comforted by the fact that we had a covering force. This, however, consisted only of one light cruiser and its destroyers, and gave us no consolation at first. We were to be very glad later that they were present.

We arrived at Empress Augusta Bay on the morning of November 8th and began unloading immediately. There was no opposition until about noon, at which time we received warning of a strong force of "Bogies" approaching from the northward. Apparently a part of this force was broken up by the Combat Air Patrol, since only about twenty of them got through. The transports got underway immediately, forming to repel attack. It was not long in developing.

The screen was first to open fire on a group of torpedo planes attempting to break into the formation. These were repelled. At nearly the same time, dive bombers began to pour out of the clouds like raindrops.

THE LADY GANGSTER

Seven peeled off and made for the *Fuller*, as the transports opened fire. We happened to be the last ship in column, and as such were a most attractive target.

One of the raiders was caught by a 3" burst and exploded before his dive had fairly begun. The other six, however, did their best to make up for the loss of their comrade. Four bombs burst in a close pattern around the ship's bow. The last of these was a near miss which perforated the side with shrapnel holes, killing one man and wounding several others. The bomber which laid this egg succumbed to a concentrated burst of fire from the 20mms and crashed in flames on the starboard bow.

The other two made for the after part of the ship. The first bomb, badly aimed, landed some distance in the wake of the ship. The final bomb, however, was far more destructive than the concentrated fury of the preceding six combined. It hit number four 3" gun, ricocheted through the after battery splinter shield, and went sailing down the ladder to the crew's compartment, where it exploded halfway to its destination.

It was lucky for the ship that the bomb ricocheted, otherwise it would have exploded in the after magazine, causing an explosion from which the ship could not possibly have survived.

My father's account matched the ship's, but also included two additional observations: *The concussions from the bombs, even the near misses, were extremely strong. The gunner nearest me was sucked out of his harness and was tossed like a rag doll, landing upside-down and wedged in the ladder above his position. I turned and saw, or felt, the blast that hit us to the rear. One of the gun crew was below the aft gun's deck platform loading shells and was blown up into the overhang. How he lived I don't know.*

That fortunate gunner was Elgin Bowen. He describes the blast as follows: *I was a gunner's mate assigned to the aft gun deck and was under the gun platform loading the 60-round magazines. When the bomb went off, I was thrown upward against the bottom of the gun platform. I was knocked unconscious. When I woke up, I didn't know what had happened. I didn't even hear the bomb. I was on the deck, surrounded by 20mm rounds that were rolling about. The ladder to the gun deck was blown away and I saw that the barrel of the 3" gun was bent in a hooked position. The bomb bounced off the barrel and went through a corner of the after gun deck and exploded two decks below. My shoulder and arm were hurt and I had difficulty in taking my helmet off. It was bent and dented. The blast had jammed me up into the overhead, and my helmet and the collar of my life vest cushioned the blow; they saved my life.*

Returning to the ship's account:

A fire was started in the magazine which was promptly squelched by flooding. All gear in the crew's compartment was destroyed; and all steam and water lines in that area, as well as electrical leads, were demolished. Seven men were killed by this explosion, and approximately thirty wounded. Damage control parties and medical parties swung into action immediately.

Meanwhile, the attack had somewhat tapered off. Another sporadic torpedo attack was beaten off by the destroyer screen, which also knocked down several of the attacking dive bombers which, having completed their runs, were endeavoring to escape through the formation. The flagship, USS *President Jackson*, had taken a 500 pound bomb. It hit #4 kingpost, ricocheted on the deck, and by some whim of providence, failed to explode. It was promptly thrown over the side. This, and the damage to the *Fuller*, were the only hits scored by the Japanese that day.

At the end of the attack, the formation returned to the transport area, and resumed debarkation of troops and unloading. As the day drew to a close, the reports of readiness to get underway began to go to the flag, and lo, the name of the *Fuller* led all the rest! Our damage control parties had done their work with amazing competence and speed, while the deck divisions continued unloading as before, with all hands trying to compensate for the loss of their shipmates by doing more than their share.

Three years previous to the day's events, the *Fuller's* crew members had still been reservists anxiously waiting for the call to duty. When my father shared the events of that day, I marveled at how complete the transformation of the Chicago Boys had been. On fire and with extensive damage, *The Gangster* shot down three dive bombers and still completed her mission—ahead of schedule!

Breaks were few and far between for the hard working Chicago Boys.

Chapter 21

Giving and Getting at Christmas – December 1943

"What was it like after the bombing and losing those men?" I just had to know.

We were back at it in less than a week. Repairs were completed at Tulagi and we just "got back on the horse," so to speak. There was nothing else to do but keep doing what we were good at. We got by with our patches until things cooled down a bit at Bougainville, and then we were sent to New Zealand again, for repairs. That was to be our last time at that wonderful place. This time we put in at Auckland instead of Wellington.

In a couple of weeks we were running supplies again in the Solomons. On Christmas Day we were replacing the Marines on Bougainville with Army units; that's when we got some great news. We were going home. Two years after leaving Norfolk and finally we were going home!

As Master at Arms I was supposed to crack down on the homemade booze, but that day I didn't care. After we did our jobs, the home-brewed stuff was everywhere. Guys were singing and dancing with each other and celebrating for quite some time.

A more sedate description comes from the ship's account:

```
Our orders required us to return to the
Solomons area, which by this time we had
come to regard as our personal and private
property. Starting again from Guadalcanal
we went up the "slot" once more, destina-
tion Bougainville. This was to be the nature
of a Christmas present for the embattled
Marines on that island. We were to arrive
on Christmas Day, with a relieving force of
Army troops, to evacuate the Marines. "All
very well and proper, for the Marines,"
thought we, "but how about us?" If we don't
return to the United States pretty soon,
```

that country will be minus some citizens of long standing. We'll have to fill out immigration papers, if and when we got back.

Christmas Day 1943 was no different than any other blitz day to us, that is until about noon. We breakfasted early in anticipation of early general quarters, and with a long day of hard work ahead.

Unloading progressed in its usual swift and efficient manner until just before noon. At that time, the ship's loudspeaker system blared: "This is the Commanding Officer speaking. You men have done a fine job today as in the past. I want to thank you for that." (An audible groan arose.)

"And now, I have a little Christmas present for you." (Silence.)

"The *Fuller* has been ordered to return to the United States."

The blast of cheering which followed this startled all the sea gulls within a five-mile radius. Equipment and cargo disappeared from the holds and reappeared on the beach with truly amazing speed, and long before nightfall the ship was empty of Army troops and cargo and was loaded with Marines."

The Gangster and its Chicago Boys were going home!

Chapter 22

Much Needed Repairs for the Lady and Her Men

When we reached anchorage in San Francisco's harbor on January 17, 1944, the ship was immediately scheduled for an extensive overhaul in Mare Island Navy Yard, and we crew members were granted much needed, and long overdue, leave.

"What was it like to come home after such a long time, and after so many happenings?" My mind raced through the events I had learned of while driving and I was trying to sort them all out. I wondered what it could have been like for those young men from Chicago to come home after three years of travel, adventure, and change. America was fighting in the Pacific and planning for the invasion of Europe with a total of over nine million men and women in uniformed service. Although the economy was over-heated due to war production, rationing was imposed. Items such as meat, butter, sugar, gasoline, and car tires were in short supply. The war had touched every part of life.

Everything at home was different. My marriage was over. The war had been both its cause and end.

He said no more about it, and I did not ask. Later, as an adult, I learned some of the details, and we discussed the experience. True to his nature, he remained a gentleman.

Home looked the same at first. The familiar streets and houses of Blue Island were all there, but soon I noticed that everything was either better or worse than I remembered. It was winter, and after two years of living and working in the tropics, I was cold like never before. I wanted to relax, to be quiet. But that was impossible.

Everyone wanted to know things about the war. They were constantly asking questions and, at first, I somehow resented it. Then, I realized what had happened. I was the news. For the people at home everything about the war was "out there," and I was part of it. My coming home personally brought "out there" to them.

Life magazine had a spread on the Bougainville invasion and I was surprised to find the Fuller in one of the photos. It seemed unreal. I read the article, and it was a fair description as far as it went. But, there's no way to tell folks at home about the war. You have to be there to understand it.

The war was very different on the home front. The newspapers, radio, and magazines told about a world-wide war. People at home saw a much wider view. All I really knew about was the Fuller's *war. My war was smaller.*

I could not get comfortable with all the questions. They wanted to know, but I really couldn't tell them everything I knew.

It was during this leave when my father had remained tight-lipped with the reporter. He told me that the instruction to "keep quiet about things while at home" was taken seriously by those servicemen who had seen real action. They knew firsthand the price paid by men in harm's way. They kept quiet.

Also, I knew that leave was not forever. I wanted to get back to the Fuller. *We had to finish a job much bigger than when we started. I found it uncomfortable to think about life at home knowing that it was not available until the war was over.*

When his leave ended, my father returned to San Francisco and found that things had also changed aboard *The Gangster*. Less than half of the approximately 300 reservists who commissioned the *Fuller* were still aboard in early 1944. The Navy was expanding at considerable speed and needed experienced sailors for the vast number of vessels being churned out of shipyards. The Chicago Boys advanced in rank at the cost of finding themselves transferred. On the newer ships, they were now "the Salts."

My father had many cousins living in and near Chicago; none were more lovely than Ann Staecker, who was a favorite of my father (right) and his brother Vernon. Soon after this reunion, in February 1944, my uncle was headed to Europe in the Army and my father (by then a Salt) was back on *The Gangster*.

My father told me more about his trip home: *Your Uncle Art was transferred off the ship in 1943. Our furloughs crossed in 1944 and we were together at home for a few days, and then I didn't see him again until after the war. A lot of the guys went to newer ships as petty officers, or to schools as instructors. I was relieved when I learned I was staying on the* Fuller. *I was promoted to Bosun's Mate First Class in '44.*

While home on leave, my father (left) got an opportunity to inspect his prized possession—a 1940 Oldsmobile. His brother Vernon is with him.

On the *Fuller*, the remaining original crew members became the senior enlisted men who would guide a refurbished *Gangster* as part of a greatly expanded Amphibious Force. Here is the ship's description:

> Now began a new era for the *Fuller*. For the past two years we had been used to getting along on a shoestring...or rather, to be more exact, a half shoestring. There had been very little in the way of protection in the South Pacific for the few auxiliaries which had been instrumental in building up the United States' bases in the Solomons and in New Guinea. While we lay in Mare Island undergoing repairs, the mighty Amphibious Force, and the rejuvenated Battle Force, made the landings in the Gilberts and in the Marshall Islands. It was evident that, however valuable the lessons in amphibious warfare which had been assembled with so much painstaking care by ships like the *Fuller* in the South and Southwest Pacific, new difficulties were apt to arise in the more northern and coral atolls like the Marshall and Gilbert Islands. Most of these were resolved after the difficulty at Tarawa, and the information gained was disseminated throughout the Amphibious Force.

My father described the distinct difference he saw in the Navy after the *Fuller* left San Francisco: *The training and maneuvers we did in early 1944 were bigger and longer than everything before. We went to San Diego and then on to Pearl Harbor. We practiced landings in Hawaii, and everywhere we went there seemed to be men, ships, and equipment. It made what we did in the Solomons look like a sideshow.*

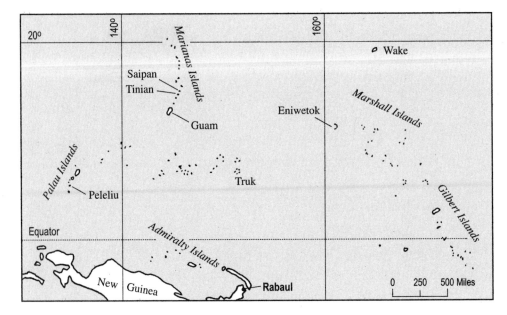

Eniwetok and Saipan

Chapter 23

Saipan and the New War

My promotion to become a first class bosun meant another change in duty. I was no longer Master at Arms. During my time on the Fuller *I had acquired experience in many of the different areas of troop operations. I could handle all the duties involved in loading, unloading, and recovering troops. When we left Hawaii, I was assigned to lead one of the beach details. Next time, I was going ashore with the Marines.*

My father eased back as I drove. He was thinking about something serious. I felt that if I was patient I would hear something important. I let him take his time. He was remembering Saipan.

From the ship's account:

> We arrived in Eniwetok on the eighth of June, and gasped at what we saw there. There were battleships, carriers, and cruisers in numbers which to us were astronomical. Auxiliaries and destroyers uncountable! We lay in Eniwetok, marveling, for three days, then got underway on June 11th 1944 with a force even larger than that with which we had come in. And, wonder of wonders, there were three escort carriers giving us a constant Combat Air Patrol. Even though we were going to blitz Saipan, we felt safe as in church after having seen that display of power, and knowing that the battle force was ahead of us, taking care of any opposition which might present itself.

My father spoke: *Saipan was supposed to be easy. At least that's what we were told as we headed there. We were in a large convoy and that made us feel very safe. The force going into Saipan was tremendous compared to Guadalcanal and Bougainville. But, I had no idea how dangerous it was going to be. My new assignment put me on the beach full time during landings.*

At Saipan we were given a special mission. The Fuller *was part of a fake invasion. Everything went well at first. We fooled the Japs, and then....*

He trailed off and I could feel him disappear to another time and place.

From the ship's account:

We arrived off Saipan in the early morning of June fifteenth. Standing into transport area our division formed with Transport Division 10 and other units, a demonstration group 52.9 under Captain G.D. Morrison, to make a feint at Beaches Black 1 and 2, and Scarlet 1 and 2. We slowed, lowered boats, and dispatched landing craft towards the beach. Meanwhile the main force had arrived off the southern end of the island, and were doing the same. They, however, were not faking. The purpose of our feint was to draw some of the opposition from the main landing beaches to the northern end of the island. The measure of its success may be judged by a broadcast from Radio Tokyo, to the effect that a large landing force had been repulsed by Saipan's "heroic defenders" at Garapan [on Saipan's northern tip] .

My father came back to his story.

I was not with the Fuller *for the fake landing. Our beach detail was off-loaded to another ship. We went in with their Marines as part of the real invasion.*

He stopped again. I waited, then asked, "You mean coming off a

112

Higgins boat like the Marines?"

Not just like them. We were with them, but in the second or third wave. At least I didn't have to go in as part of the very first wave. Navy or Marines, coming off the boats, you all look the same to the Japs. We had it bad, but the Marines took it head on right from the start. The Japs were not going to make it easy on Saipan.

"Were you scared?" I had to ask.

Of course I was. Anyone who says they were not scared is crazy or a liar. I had dropped off plenty of Marines on Guadalcanal and Bougainville and then picked up the wounded. Guys, just kids mostly, coming back all shot up. The dead didn't get picked up. I was scared all right.

Saipan had a reef just like Tarawa and getting in was not easy. We had to stop at the reef and re-load onto Ducks for the trip to the actual beach-head. Everyone knew about Tarawa and nerves were strained. We avoided the mistakes made at Tarawa, but there was a lot of confusion with the re-loading. The Fuller's *beach platoon got left on shore overnight.*

My father's reference to Tarawa and the transfer onto the amphibian craft known as Ducks was chilling. Duck was slang for DUKW, a six-wheel, 7.5 ton amphibious truck produced by General Motors for the purpose of transporting troops and cargo on water and/or land. The nomenclature stands for: D (a vehicle designed in 1942); U (utility-amphibious); K (all-wheel drive); W (two powered axles).

On Tarawa the U.S. lost 1,677 men in a disastrous series of errors which began with an insufficient artillery barrage. The Japanese defenders, bolstered by an elite Imperial Japanese Marine unit of 2,619 men, were well dug in and able to easily pick off the incoming Marines. The Higgins boats were stalled by a reef and men were off loaded as much as five-hundred yards away from the beach. Of the first wave, only a few men made it to the shore.

My father continued his description of his experience on Saipan: *The beach platoon was there to run the beach after it was taken. We were not sup-posed to be involved in the fight for the beach. We had some Marines with us as guards, but when we landed on the beach it hadn't been fully taken. It was touch-and-go all day. We took all kinds of fire, and all I had was a .45 caliber pistol.*

The ship's account tells of the *Fuller* rejoining the main force:

In due time, we recovered our boats, rounded southward to transport area 3, and joined the main force at the southern end of Saipan. The *Fuller* was directed to prepare its landing force. The beach platoon from the ship had previously been embarked on the squadron flagship and was even now on the beach, engaged in its assigned activities. We were assigned Beach Yellow 1 for unloading and, within a short time, unloading was well on its way. The boat crews were making their runs to the beach, which was, now that the landing point had been determined by the Japanese, under heavy mortar and machine gun fire.

As the boats returned from the beach they brought with them the casualties. In addition to the casualties brought aboard by our own boats, LST 273 came alongside with 24 badly wounded troops. These were brought aboard with all possible tenderness and taken care of by the ship's medical department. There had been no real air operation, although throughout the day warnings of "bogies" at varying distances were received. These, apparently, were well taken care of by the Combat Air Patrol, since no Japanese plane put in an appearance over Saipan. As evening approached, our squadron got underway for the night. We hoisted whatever boats happened to be in the vicinity of the ship at the time and

```
joined the formation. The remainder of the
boats were left at the island, to rejoin
the ship in the morning.
```

My father spoke about being left on the beach: *You asked if I was scared. Well yes, I was scared all day long, but you just deal with it. We came under fire from all types of weapons—rifles, machine guns, mortars, and artillery. It tapered off as the day wore on. I started to feel better until the ships pulled out for the night. Then I found out for real about being scared.*

From the *Fuller's* account:

```
As we steamed away in the growing dusk, we
could see the loom of large fires on the
beach, started by the combatant ships in
their pre-invasion bombardment, while one
or two destroyers kept the front lines illu-
minated by starshells throughout the night.
It was a lovely sight, if one happened to
be in the mood for aesthetic beauty. We
weren't. The sight of the Marine and Army
casualties which we had been receiving gave
mute evidence of the savage battle in
progress; the only visible signs of which
were the occasional tracer streaks standing
out sharply in the darkness.
```

My father told me what it was like from his point of view. *The first night on a hostile beach—just invaded by Marines—is not where a sailor like me wanted to be. I felt I'd be lucky to see the next day's light.*

A Sailor's Memoir

Chapter 24

Praying All Night for a Man to Die

I knew my father as a peace-loving man. To me he always presented the best example of living life by the dictates of the Sermon on the Mount. He seldom lost his temper, and he always went the extra mile not to offend or be offended. What he next told me was a shock.

Saipan was when I prayed all night for a man to die.

I was unable to form a question.

He could tell by my silence that I wanted to ask, so he went on without me speaking: *The ship left us. They had to. You can't sit all night off of a beach and be a target. So the* Fuller *and the other transports moved out. When that happened I got very concerned. It was my ship. My home...and it was gone. Now I knew how the troops on the beach felt after we dropped them off. At night the transports have to move. Makes sense, but it is scary when you are the one left on the beach.*

At night, the beach was a very different place. We had been moving back and forth along our part of the beach all day, trying not to be targets. We jumped in and out of foxholes and trenches and hid behind equipment. The beach was loose sand on top of coral and rock. The trenches and foxholes we dug had to be shallow because it was so hard to dig.

When the sun started to go down, a Marine who seemed in charge of a forward detachment came back to instruct all of us in the beach platoon. He told us to dig holes as fast as possible and be ready to stay in them all night. Snipers were expected. He ran forward and we never saw him again.

I began to dig. The beach was hard, and the best I could do was dig a shallow horizontal foxhole. I placed chunks of coral, rock, and equipment along the island side of the trench and hunkered down. I held my .45 and kept it outside its holster. I knew that if I was ever to need it, I'd need it fast. If the Japs pushed the Marines back, they'd be close. I prepared myself to shoot anything that didn't look like a Marine.

I finally croaked out a question. "You...you said...you said you prayed for a man to die?"

Nothing I'm proud of. He was silent.

I stayed silent also.

Then, after a long wait, he explained: *That Marine was right. When it got dark the snipers zeroed in on us. A shot hit near me. There was no way to know where they came from. All I could do was hug the bottom of my hole. I must have looked like an easy target. Maybe he thought I was an officer. We didn't wear insignias on our uniforms, and I had a side arm and guards around me during the day. Whoever was shooting at me thought I was important.*

This one guy kept aiming just at me, all the time. If I moved, even the slightest, he'd pop one at me. He came real close that first time, but I was so scared I never gave him another good chance. I didn't breathe much. I was afraid my expanded chest would make me a better target. I tried to shrink myself. The bugs came out and started in on me. I was afraid to move and I let the bugs munch and fly about. All the while he kept shooting at me.

That's when I started praying.

As the night wore on, I'd hear shots being fired at suspected sniper positions by the Marines in nearby foxholes. I prayed each time that "my guy" was the one they'd hit. I'd hear the shouts that the Marines hit one. I'd get relieved a second and then...pop! He'd send another one at me.

I prayed and prayed, all night long. I wanted that man to die. I didn't know a thing about him except that he wanted me dead. So, I paid him back the only way I could...and kept praying that he'd be killed.

It went on and on and on. All night long he chiseled away at the protection I'd built along the edge of my foxhole. Zap! Zap! Zap! He'd hit the edge and a little bit more of my barrier disappeared. I couldn't make myself smaller. I was running out of protection.

I remember looking up at the night sky. Every so often a flare would go off and the Marines would shoot up into the palm trees. Each time they shot, I prayed harder. It was a race. The Marines would get my guy or he'd chip away at my position and eventually get a good angle, a better shot...at me. Sometimes his shots zinged over me. Those weren't what worried me. As the barrier got smaller and the bullets aimed at me got closer and closer—that's what worried me.

I pulled the car over. We sat well off the road—somewhere in southern Indiana—and the world outside our car held no interest for me. I wanted to hear every detail without distractions. "I know you made it, how close did he get to you, how'd they get him, who got him?"

He sighed and then shrugged. *I don't know.*

I was frozen.

He continued: *The sun was almost up. I knew that he knew time was running out. He started firing faster. Zap! Zap! Zap! He didn't pause. Zap! Zap! Zap! He wasn't going to wait for a good shot. He was going to make one by destroying what little protection I had left. One shot creased my shirt and another hit the edge of my foxhole at what seemed the same instant. I knew the next one, or the one after that, would hit me.*

That's when the sun came up.

At once, the visibility went from that place where you can't see anything to where you can see everything. All I can remember is the sound of gunfire. It seemed that every Marine around me fired at once. They hit more than one sniper. They had to hit the one who was after me, because it was the end of me being a target. No more shots came at me.

My prayers were answered. I never felt so good and so deeply bad, and I felt them together.

Who shot him? And which one of the dead snipers was he? I can't say. All I know is that I was a moment away from being hit. It was that close.

Now, whenever I see a sunrise, I think about that morning. I've never been so glad to see the sun come up. I know how lucky I am to see sun-ups.

In the ship's account, the *Fuller's* return to position off Saipan was a routine event:

```
Early in the morning, we returned to our
former station in the transport area, and
began again the activities of the previous
day. These were identical with their pred-
ecessors and need not be repeated.
```

For my father, and the others of the beach platoon, sighting the *Fuller* was more than comforting.

Soon, after dawn, the ships came back. The Fuller *was easy to spot off shore and we let out a cheer when we saw her. The Marines had always let us know how glad they were to see the old girl, but she never looked as good as she did that morning. I've never seen a more beautiful ship. I've never seen anything that beautiful.*

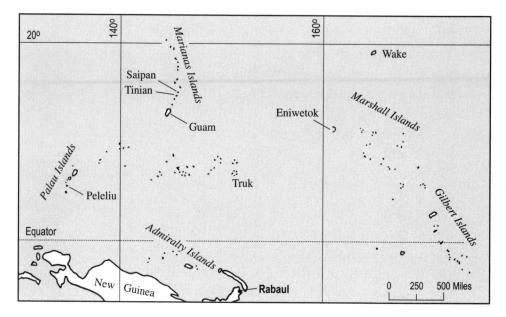

Saipan and Tinian

Chapter 25

Faking It Again, At Tinian

"How long did you stay on the beach?" I was eager to know what happened next.

A day, maybe two—time is different in situations like that. After the troops we brought in were able to secure the beachhead and move inland, we left the beach. There were always more supplies, equipment, and troops for us to deliver. We made several more runs in and out of Saipan. We even moved some prisoners.

That interested me greatly. After the night with the sniper, my father must have had strong feelings about transporting the enemy. I asked, "What were they like?"

They were small, scared, and hungry. Not at all the monsters we imagined after what we had been told.

He could tell by my expression that his answer was not what I expected. *They looked like children. Compared to us Americans, they were tiny; most didn't weigh much more than a hundred pounds. They were really underfed and some had hardly any clothes.*

We hosed them down up on the deck, gave them some of our clothes, and fed them. A couple days earlier they were trying to blow our heads off, but I couldn't stay mad at them. They had been told we'd torture and kill them if they were caught, and they looked terrified. Some wouldn't eat. They thought we were going to poison them. I felt pity for them. We transferred all of them, about fifty or sixty, to a ship-of-the-line and headed back to Saipan. And there, we saw more than we were supposed to; at least we were not supposed to talk about it.

"I don't understand; what did you see?"

Suicide Cliff, or Bonsai Cliff—take your pick of names for the place. It got those names from people jumping to their deaths rather than surrendering. The civilians were brainwashed just like the troops. I saw them jump. Some of the mothers tossed their kids. It was terrible.

Saipan was the first island that also contained civilians. During the last days of the battle, Lieutenant General Yoshitsugu Saito organized a suicidal bonsai charge made up of soldiers and civilians, whom he had convinced that it was preferable to die in combat than be taken prisoners by the hideous and barbaric U.S. forces. Hundreds of civilians also committed suicide by leaping off the island's cliffs. Twenty-two thousand civilians, many of them children, died on Saipan.

My father was silent a long time before he continued. *Saipan was short and bloody. The closer we got to Japan, the worse it was. The casualty rate for us was near twenty percent. But before we knew it, we were at it again. The Fuller was asked to pull off another fake invasion.*

The second time we fooled them was at Tinian. It was at Tinian that I almost got killed a second and then a third time.

"Snipers?" I thought of his night on Saipan. My attention was riveted to his explanation.

No. Not snipers. It was machine guns and rifles during the second attempted fake landing. We rushed the beach again like it was the actual landing spot, and the Japs let loose with all they had. Bullets were flying all around me—but none as close as on Saipan.

The third time it was a mine. After the fake landing, we went in for real just like on Saipan. When we got to the beach our landing craft exploded. All of the beach party got out. It was a miracle we weren't killed. Again, we were lucky.

Up and down the beach the rumors spread about us. Marines said we were safe because we were from the Fuller. The Gangster was a lucky ship and in their view she protected us. In the boats and on the beach the Fuller's luck stuck with us.

Time and again we avoided the worst of what was happening. There was no reason other than her luck. The Fuller and her crew were plain lucky indeed.

Again, the ship's "semi-official" account of the *Fuller's* Saipan to Tinian duty mirrored his memory:

We reappeared in the Saipan area on the 19th and immediately unloaded our cargo. In our absence, the greater part of the island had been secured by the Marines and the

Army, and they began the reduction of the nearby island of Tinian by artillery fire, which was being supplemented, when we arrived, by naval gunfire. The noise was terrific.

We received orders to load combat troops of the 2nd Marine Division and equipment, which we did in record time. We then proceeded to the long awaited invasion of Tinian. Tinian is only three miles from the south coast of Saipan, and therefore very little in the way of U.S. troop movements could be concealed from the surrounding hills. Deception was, therefore, the order of the day. In view of our previous success in the line of feinting, our division was ordered to repeat the tactics of the Saipan invasion.

In the early morning of July 24th, Task Group 52.8, of which we were a part, appeared off Blue Beach near Tinian Town on the south coast of Tinian Island. Here was the only really suitable beach for amphibious landings, a fact which the Japanese had certainly noted. To the tune of a mighty bombardment by the guns of the battleship *Colorado*, several cruisers and destroyers, we put boats into the water and dispatched them toward the beach.

The Japs were fighting with all weapons at their command. Shore batteries, well concealed in the hills, were replying to the

guns of our ships. One salvo of apparently
6" caliber scored hits on the *Colorado*,
which moved leisurely out of range, continuing to fire with clock-like regularity. As
the boat waves approached the beach they
were subjected to heavy enemy fire. They
spread out, zigzagged, and kept going right
on to their beach.

Meanwhile, the main landing was in progress
on the northern end of the island. The Japs
had been pulled so far out of position by
our feint on the southern end of the island
that all they could bring to bear on the
narrow, exposed, main landing were small
caliber guns and a few mortars. The beachhead there was made with few casualties.
Our feint successful, we recalled our
boats, hoisted them aboard, and joined the
main force. In due time we sent our troops
ashore and unloaded our cargo. The DUKW
carrying our beach platoon to the beach
struck a mine just as she was beaching and
was destroyed, although the beach party
miraculously escaped.

The fighting on Tinian mirrored that on its sister island of Saipan.
The Japanese retreated by day and attacked aggressively at night. For
the first time in the war, napalm was used to dislodge defenders.

Tinian was strategically very important for the Allied forces. The
island was needed as a launching site for the aerial assault on Japan.
Six runways, over a mile-and-a—half in length, were constructed for
the new B-29 Super Fortress bombers, and over 50,000 support troops
were stationed on Tinian after it was subdued.

Yet, for the invading Marines and the crews of the APAs that supported them, Tinian was another routine mission. My father, like all the men on site, saw it in personal terms: *I sure was lucky not to have been killed on Tinian.*

His tone and temperament had changed, and I sensed that he was becoming uncomfortable remembering this part of his experiences. Maybe he should stop.

As I drove I realized that my previous exposure to this part of America's history had been superficial. It had mainly come through war books, movies, and the occasional TV or newspaper retrospective on an anniversary of D-Day or the nuclear bombs dropping on Japan. My father was an eyewitness—and I pressed him. "Dad, what was it really like?"

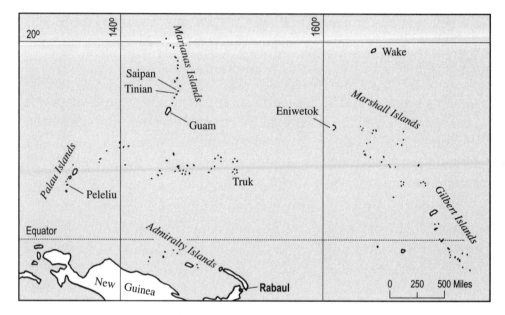

Saipan, Tinian, and Peleliu

Chapter 26

Just Another Invasion

He did not answer immediately. I sensed that he would have preferred not telling me, but my father was an honest man. I believe he wanted me to know, perhaps as a means of avoidance of such things in my life. He clearly had no use for war's perceived glory.

My job with the beach platoon put me right on the beach into operations with the Marines. The three landings I did with the beach detail were real quick. Saipan, Tinian, and then Peleliu were back-to-back-to-back. Let me tell you, there's absolutely nothing good about war. The only positive thing is the end.

It was not good on those islands. It never was anything good. The war in the Pacific can't ever be seen as anything other than madness.

He halted, took a deep breath, and then continued: *That morning on Saipan, when I got through praying all night for that sniper to get killed, I saw bodies hanging from the palm trees. The snipers didn't fall out of the trees when they were shot. They couldn't. They tied themselves to the trees. So in the morning their bodies just hung there in the sun.*

It was horrible. The stench of death hung over everything on those islands.

The Japanese troops lived mostly on rice, and their starch diet caused their corpses to decompose faster than our troops. We didn't cut them down right away. We had more important things to do. Our wounded and dead came first. But, we learned you had to cut the Japs down soon or the hanging bodies would bloat up and rupture. Maggots were everywhere and they'd even come down like rain when a dead sniper exploded.

Saipan and Tinian were bad, but Peleliu...it was the worst. We were led to believe that the war was turning in our favor. Maybe it was. But on those islands, it was anything but. Off shore it looked easier. As part of the beach party, I was in it closer and longer than I care to remember. The Japs dug in and fought hard. They chewed up our troops. On the Fuller, *we took whole young men in to the beaches and brought out pieces. It was worse than terrible.*

My father's comments concerning his experiences on these islands were very disturbing to me at the time. Peleliu was particularly horrendous and for inexplicable reasons has not received its due attention over the years. Perhaps it was so horrific that collectively the military and our society at large wishes to forget. Even so near an observer as Albert C. Allen described it as "just another invasion" in the ship's account.

The campaign on Peleliu, Operation Stalemate II, was well named. It has become the Forgotten Battle of the Pacific War. In some opinions, it was America's hardest fought and most difficult engagement in all of World War II. It was on Peleliu that the Japanese perfected their new defense tactics.

No longer would the Japanese seriously defend the landing beaches. After experiencing heavy aerial and naval bombardments, they chose to lightly defend the beaches and instead withdraw to fortified positions inland. Also, the suicidal banzai charges, such as those first attempted on Guadalcanal, were abandoned in favor of well planned, small-scale night counter attacks. The overall strategy was attrition—to bleed the invading Americans.

The Japanese had recently established the "Absolute National Defense Zone," and Peleliu was an important position on its perimeter. It was to be held at all costs. The Japanese military leadership vowed that it was not to be lost. With a total of approximately 38,000 men on and around Peleliu, the Japanese defensive force almost equaled the U.S. invasion force of 47,561 soldiers and Marines. Peleliu, and its neighboring islands, would be strongly defended since "fighting to the end" remained the overall and final premise for all of the Japanese defenders.

The hellish details of Peleliu cannot be recounted in full here. But one statistic may adequately describe the ferocity of the battle. By the end of September 20, 1944, the fifth day of fighting, the battle-tested 1st Marine Division suffered 1,749 casualties. That amount is only six fewer than the total received by that unit in its six-months-long assignment at Guadalcanal. The large number of casualties caused the 1st Marines to be replaced by the 321st Regimental Combat Team of the Army's 81st Infantry Division and may be one reason that the battle has

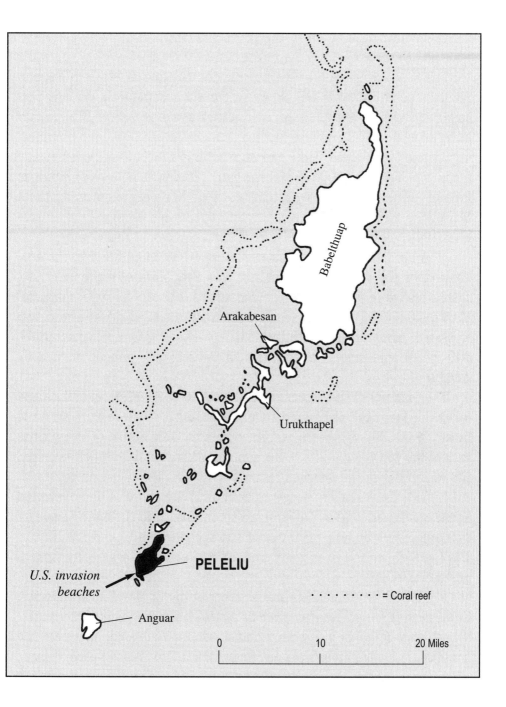

Babelthuap

Arakabesan

Urukthapel

U.S. invasion beaches **PELELIU**

· · · · · · · · · · = Coral reef

Anguar

0   10   20 Miles

not received notice equal to the perceived "all Marine" efforts of Iwo Jima and Okinawa.

The best description of the horrendous fighting is found in Eugene Sledge's book, *With the Old Breed: At Peleliu and Okinawa*. In this personal account he writes, it was a "nether world of horror from which escape seemed less and less likely as casualties mounted and the fighting dragged on and on. Time had no meaning; life had no meaning. The fierce struggle made savages of us all." The men he served with on Peleliu "suffered so much for their country. None came out unscathed. Many gave their lives, their health and some their sanity. All who survived will long remember the horror that they would rather forget."

The human cost on Peleliu was staggering. In addition to the decimation of the 1st Marine Division, the 7th Marines suffered 1,497 casualties while the 5th Marines' casualties reached 1,378. In total, the Marines endured 4,624 dead, 36 missing (presumed dead) and 5,450 wounded. Army units also suffered heavy losses with 1,393 casualties, 208 killed, on Peleliu and 1,614 casualties, 260 killed, on nearby Angaur.

The tenacity of the defense was the cause of the high casualties and for it the Japanese paid dearly. Only a pittance of the defending force lived. Of the 202 prisoners taken on Peleliu, only nineteen were members of the Japanese military. Korean and Okinawan laborers comprised the remainder of the surviving group.

In fact, the Japanese desire to hold until the end was demonstrated in the continued hold-out of isolated small groups in the mountains and swamps of Peleliu long after defeat and the war's end. On April 22nd of 1947, an officer and twenty-six soldiers and eight sailors finally surrendered on Peleliu.

My father continued his frank description: *It was hot, always hot. Those islands looked beautiful from off shore on a ship. But in the war, there was no such thing as a tropical paradise. Once you landed, they were just hot, diseased, and bug-infested hell holes. When it gets warm each summer, my feet break out again with "jungle rot" that I picked up then. You can't get rid of it.*

That point was well known to me. I learned early that my father's

"Hell on earth," is how my father described island warfare. "Heat, grime, bugs, and the smell of death," is all that he recalled. Perhaps the Marines on Peleliu saw the worst conditions in the Pacific Theater.

shoes were off- limits for "dress up" play as a child. Each summer I saw him suffer through painful episodes with his distressed feet.

He continued: *We'd deliver fresh troops and right away you saw the toll those places took on them. In a day or less, we'd start taking out the wounded. The wounded always came first. If they made it back to the beach, we'd rush them out to a ship. A lot of them never made it to where we could help them. Bodies were stacked up like cords of wood. On those islands, the dead had to wait.*

We got to the dead when we could. Our troops were buried in as decent a manner as possible. The heat and the flies pushed us to take care of them as quickly as possible. They deserved better, but all that could be done for them was to lay them out and cover them up. At least they were identified and marked. The Japs weren't.

Because there were so many, the enemy dead were buried differently. Large holes were bulldozed, and they were put in and covered as quickly as possible. There was little more we could do because of the numbers. It was terrible, and the worst of what I can remember is the smell. Your memory can't get rid of it. It's like jungle rot in your brain.

He stopped talking then and stayed silent for quite some time. I continued to drive. I did not understand fully at the time but, years later, when I encountered Sledge's book, I recalled my father's silence.

Sledge's words about the horror of it all were true.

Chapter 27

Doing It Twice In the Philippines

Compared to Peleliu, the Philippines were nothing. We got two campaign ribbons for them because such a big deal was made over MacArthur and his return to the Philippines. The landings were easy. We ran in and out of there several times, always with a lot of ships. There were more and more ships in 1944.

We had great air cover, but the Japs were beginning to break through every so often with suicide planes. They never came near to us on these two operations. But one of the ships close to us did get hit. The ship that got hit had taken our place in the formation at the last minute. Again, the Fuller *was lucky.*

Planes were one thing. At least we could see them. We were more worried about the subs. The waters around the Philippines were filled with them.

"What about torpedoes?"

Yes, we certainly saw torpedoes. Once, two were shot at us at the same time. One was headed for the bow and the other nearer the stern. The Captain ordered the helmsman to turn right toward them. He narrowed our profile as a target by steering between the two of them. They passed on either side of us. I was on deck and watched one pass on the starboard side and then I ran across to see the wake of the other one passing on the port. That was some maneuver!

For my father, the Philippines were a big deal only because General MacArthur's ego was wrapped up in returning to the site of his less-than-heroic retreat in 1941. I believe my father discounted his own role in these invasions because they were not as brutally violent as the previous landings and because he disliked MacArthur.

As I drove, my father shared a great number of details about the invasions and related naval actions. His memory is validated by the ship's account. It is an excellent recapping of what had truly become old hat for the *Fuller* and her crew.

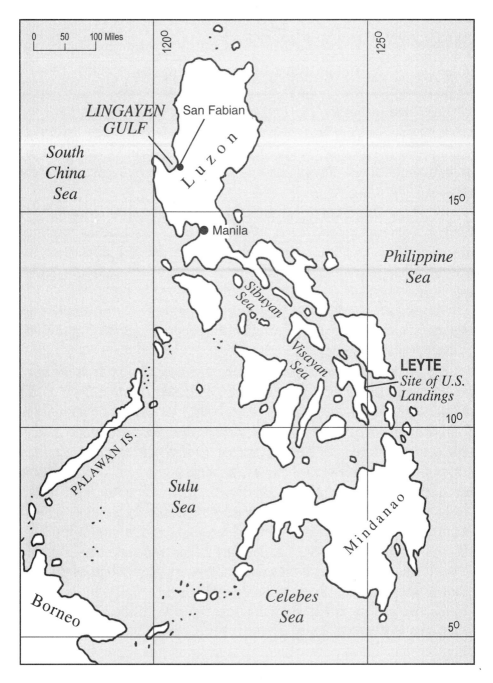

Philippine Islands

Events were moving with great rapidity now, and with great forces at the disposal of the high command, there was no delay in making invasion after invasion.

We left Hollandia on the 13th of October in company with Task Unit 78.1.3, bound, at last, for the Philippines. The trip through seas once tightly bound by Jap sea and air-power was comparatively uneventful. Several "bogies" put in an appearance, but these were promptly shot down by the Combat Air Patrol, and but for the fact that they undoubtedly reported our force, they did no damage.

The Seventh Fleet struck Leyte on the 20th of October, our boats among the thousands of others. The Japanese, expecting our forces to hit Mindanao, were caught off balance by the strike at the Visayan Islands, and the landing was made against only sporadic resistance. Small formations of Jap planes made ineffectual raids against the ships in the bay, but they did no damage, and were nearly all shot down by the covering aircraft, or by the tremendous volume of anti-aircraft fire which arose from the hundreds of ships, including that of the *Fuller* lost amid the bursts which darkened the sky.

This armada, with huge numbers and devastating firepower, is a far cry from the thirteen transports which comprised the amphibious force that 26 months earlier had invaded Guadalcanal. The *Fuller* unloaded

her troops and cargo, even more rapidly than her usual, and was gone
before nightfall.

During our five-day run back to Hollandia,
the combat ships of the Seventh and Third
Fleets intercepted the bulk of the Japanese
Navy, and in the now-famous Second Battle
of the Philippine Sea, sent their ragged
remnants scurrying back to the safety of
Japan. The back of Japan's sea power was
now broken, and we knew that the worst we
now would have to contend with would be her
dwindling air force.

On the return run from Hollandia, a lone
plane pierced the air cover net and turned
attention away from the ever-present subs.
This run was not as uneventful as the previous one, for the escorting destroyers
were kept busy fighting off Japanese submarines, and one day out of Leyte, a Jap
torpedo bomber tried to sneak into the formation and plant his fish. He came from the
starboard side, and apparently changing his
mind about his target, swung along the
length of the convoy to the rear, and made
his run on one of the LSVs (*Catskill*) which
was bringing up the rear. His torpedo
missed, and he ran into a burst from his
target which knocked him into the water.
The *Catskill* was given credit for knocking
him down.

We anchored in Leyte on the 14th, in the
middle of an air raid. A group of five

Zeroes, perhaps the escort of a bombing force which had been cut to shreds, were roaring around the harbor, with an equal number of P-38s after them. They joined their ancestors promptly, three by the fire of the P-38s, and the remainder by the guns of the surface forces.

Once again, the *Fuller* off-loaded troops and cargo in record time. She left the "hot area" on the day of arrival, accomplishing her task in five hours and twenty-six minutes. On her return trip from Ataipe, New Guinea, subs and suicide planes were about.

We left Ataipe on the 28th (December), in company with U.S.S. *Blue Ridge* (Fleet Guide and OTC), plus units of Task Group 78.1 and escorts. Our trip north as far as Leyte was quiet. We did not stop there, but turned through the passage between Leyte and Mindanao, and entered the Sulu Sea. From this point onward, our force, and the one astern of us were beset by Jap aircraft, which had by now gotten into the habit of making suicide attacks. Japan's submarines were quite active, for in the narrow passages between the islands of the Philippines group, there is marvelous hunting for a well-manned submarine.

On January 9th the *Fuller* dropped her Higgins boats in Lingayen Gulf at Luzon for a second invasion on the Philippines and the seventh assault landing of her career, not counting the friendly invasion of Iceland. The ship's account described it:

Standing into transport area Able off San
Fabian, and swung into the routine of the
"Amphibs." The first wave of troops left
the ship at 1056, followed by two waves
leaving at one minute intervals and hit the
beach without too much opposition, thanks to
the accuracy of the bombardment. We remained
in Lingayen that night, getting little
sleep, due to the almost constant presence
of suicide aircraft over the gulf, and to
the fact that we still had some cargo to
unload, not having received our unloading
orders until late in the evening. We had
completed debarkation by daylight, despite
the interruptions, and were able, on the
tenth, to retire from the area with our
group. For the prompt unloading of the ship
during difficult conditions, and in such
short time, Captain Pigman was awarded a
citation (letter of commendation) from 7th
Fleet.

Having completed unloading, we got underway
at 1803 for Leyte, Philippines Islands, in
company with a formation under command of
U.S.S. *Cavalier* (APA 37 and OTC) and U.S.S.
DuPage (APA 41 and formation guide). Due to
a last minute change in plan, we were
relieved as column leader by the *DuPage*. At
1917 one enemy aircraft was sighted dead
ahead coming in low and at 1918 this plane
was seen to crash into the *DuPage*. The
DuPage was lit up momentarily by a tremendous explosion. There were many casualties.
Survivors were sighted in the water, and we,

```
as well as the ships following us, maneu-
vered to avoid these, meanwhile dropping
life jackets and rings to those in the
water.
```

Had she held her original position the *Fuller*, rather than the *DuPage*, would have been hit. As my father said, *The Gangster's* incredible luck held. By February 1945 she was in the Carolines training troops for what would earn her a ninth battle star and prove to be the last great invasion of the war—Okinawa.

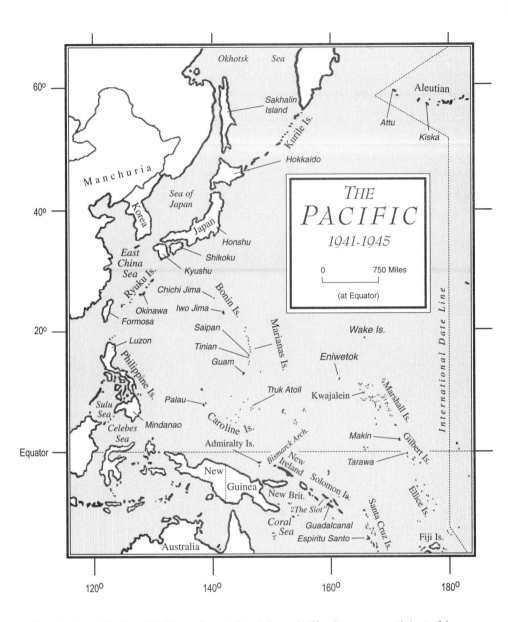

Beginning with the Allied invasion at Guadalcanal, *The Gangster* participated in many of the major campaigns and battles that forced Imperial Japan's evacuation of the South Pacific. Note the proximity of Okinawa to Japan.

Chapter 28

A Sitting Duck at Okinawa

My father disliked most movies about the war. In his opinion
Hollywood almost always sacrificed the truth. However, he did grudg-
ingly give an okay to the popular and reasonably faithful 1943 version
of *Guadalcanal Diary*, and also to James Cagney's portrayal of Admiral
Halsey in *The Gallant Hours*. Like every kid in my generation, I had seen
John Wayne's performance in *The Sands of Iwo Jima* at least a dozen
times. On this trip, my father exposed me to the nature of war in the
Pacific, and I would forever be disappointed in that film's portrayal of
the war. Still, I had to ask, "Did the *Fuller* land Marines at Iwo Jima?"

*No, we didn't. We went to Okinawa instead. Both invasions were large
operations requiring a lot of preparation. If you went to one, you missed the
other. We drew Okinawa and not Iwo Jima.*

For Okinawa, the Fuller *took on board a special unit for delivery ashore.
Maybe that's why we went there. It was a Marine aviation outfit, and we had
to wait off shore a while to land them. We sat off shore for days and days
waiting for the spot designated for an airfield to be taken by the landing
force.*

*It's a miracle one of the Kamikazes didn't land on us while we waited.
They tried damn hard. We were sitting ducks for almost a week.*

*None of us slept much that whole time. I spent all that week on deck
spotting planes and directing gunners. Maybe the higher-ups thought they
were doing us a favor after Saipan, Tinian, and Peleliu by giving us a break
from the initial landing. But it was no favor.*

*We were on constant alert and always at our battle stations under
"General Quarters." I think we fired our guns more in that operation than the
rest of the entire war.*

Okinawa was the site of the heaviest suicide attacks of the war.
Again, the *Gangster's* luck was strong. The ship's account tells of the
eight days under air attack off Bolo Point:

Suicidal kamikaze planes descended in swarms at Okinawa.

Easter Day, 1945, was also April Fool's Day. For all the forces in the vicinity of Okinawa, it was a day for neither rejoicing nor for foolishness. At about 0700 that morning, the first wave of Army and Marines hit Okinawa's beaches and began the bloody struggle for that island, the winning of which was one of the deciding blows of this long and heartbreaking war. We had embarked a Marine Air Group, and since it was not planned to beach these men until their assigned airfield had been well secured, the *Fuller* was engaged in the unaccustomed business of lying idle while her companions put troops ashore on a hostile beach. So we sat, with boats aboard, near point "Bolo" and watched the show from a ringside seat. We didn't like it. All our previous training and instincts told us to get those men ashore and get out of the area before we were sorry. But there we remained for eight

THE LADY GANGSTER

long days and nights, while suicide planes came over us, looking for a nice juicy target. During the night attacks, we were shrouded in smoke, and during the day our guns banged away at those planes which came within range.

It was on the sixth of April that the Japanese made a mighty strike at the shipping assembled around Okinawa. The Combat Air Patrol shot down Japs by the dozens, but they came on in droves. The brunt of the attack was borne by the destroyers, destroyer escorts, and the smaller pickets, which were placed at varying distances on all sides of the island. Many of these valiant craft were hit, and some were sunk, but with their anti-aircraft batteries they ran up a bag of Japs which first equaled, and finally surpassed that of the aircraft. Comparatively few Japanese lived to reach the transport area. Those which did were promptly shot down by the guns of the auxiliaries. One which will remain in the memories of the men of the *Fuller* came in from the northward and was taken under fire by this ship as it came into range. The accuracy of the fire dissuaded him from completing the run he had begun on us, and he veered to his right, lost altitude, and crashed into the water in the vicinity of a group of LSTs. It is quite possible that he was shot down by this ship, but a kill for us was not claimed since the LSTs were

143

firing at him at the same time. That, however, was unimportant. The real victory was in the fact that he caused no damage to anyone.

On the evening of the 7th, the word at last came over that we were to debark the air group. We moved south off of the Hogushi Beaches and begun unloading immediately, and with a will; all hands wanted nothing more than to get away from the area on the double.

My father explained the ordeal: *The air alerts were almost constant. They weren't trying to bomb or strafe us. Their planes attacked in only one way—suicide runs. A lot of ships were hit [223 in total] and more than a couple dozen [thirty-six] sank off Okinawa. Later we heard that, for the first time, they even planned to use suicide boats; three hundred fifty such boats were found at Kamara Island and destroyed before being used. When we finally got word to get those Marine aviators ashore, we did it in record time, even for us.*

Upon leaving Okinawa, the *Fuller* had completed its most protracted and intense period of combat in what had been a full year of constant amphibious operations. My father had a favorite expression for being tired.

He said, *We were pooh'd-out, no other word for it. We were just pooh'd-out.*

On May 11, 1945, while supporting the Okinawa invasion, the USS *Bunker Hill* was hit by two suicide planes within thirty seconds. It was the single worst kamikaze attack and resulted in 346 dead, 43 missing, and 264 wounded sailors. Although seriously crippled, the *Bunker Hill* remained afloat.

This is a typical view from the helm area of a Higgins boat as the craft approaches a beach during an invasion landing.

Chapter 29

"Surprise!"

Just when you think you have seen it all, the Navy can actually still surprise you.

My father smiled when he resumed the *Fuller's* story after it left Okinawa.

We headed to a rear area where we fully expected to begin the usual re-supply runs to the last place where we dropped off troops. But instead we got orders to Pearl Harbor. That was a surprise. Then on the way to Pearl, we got surprised again. We were going home. Now that was a real surprise!

From the ship's semi-official account:

Arriving at Saipan on the 13th [of April], we remained there only long enough to receive orders to Pearl Harbor, and on the 15th we got underway. It was a quiet and peaceful run for two days, and then, of all things, our orders were changed to the United States. Spirits soared, and all hands turned to cleaning up ship and making plans for the coming yard period. It was badly needed, for a year of constant running, and blitzes, had worn the ship and its equipment down, to say nothing of its personnel. We arrived in Honolulu on the 26th; there we embarked casualties, Coast Guard, Marine, and Navy personnel. Finally, on May 6th we passed under the Golden Gate Bridge, to the accompaniment of cheers and whistles from everyone assembled on the deck to witness the lovely sight.

The ship was given a thorough going over in

147

the Moore Shipyards. All hands went home on long-awaited leaves while the *Fuller* was getting her face lifted. During this yard period, the command of the *Fuller* was changed again. Commander C.B. Hamblett, USNR, relieved Captain Pigman, and on the 16th of July, we were again ready to join the Fleet.

As before, we were sent to San Diego for a shakedown and training cruise, and we joined the training division for a week. The exercises this time were carried on without troops and were off Coronado rather than San Clemente. At the end of this period, we loaded up with 66 Army officers, a Naval passenger detachment, and a cargo of lumber, and left the United States on the 26th. Here followed a long run to Eniwetok, Marshall Islands, during which the Army bomber command turned loose with their fearful atomic bombs, and the Russians entered the war [against Japan]. The end was in sight!

My father's account of the last days of the war expressed some trepidation. *When we left the States, everyone was on edge. The Germans had been beat, but the Japs were another thing altogether. We were glad to know that the men and equipment from Europe would be available to help us. But, we had seen all too well how tough the Japs fought at Okinawa. Another one like that, but much larger, was hard to think about.*

We knew that the re-fitting was to get us ready for the invasion of Japan. Nobody was looking forward to it. The further the Fuller *got from home, the more serious we became.*

When rumors spread that a "super bomb" had been dropped, and then another, we hoped that an invasion of Japan would not be necessary. At that time no one criticized the decision to use atomic weapons. We all felt that far more people would have died if we had invaded. I remembered the cliffs at Saipan. I still have nightmares about what I saw.

He went silent. In the quiet I thought I heard him whisper something. I cannot swear I heard it all. But he prayed—I know that. He was dead set against war and its carnage and I heard him pray for "no more." After more silence, he resumed.

You can say what you want about Harry Truman, but you can't fault him for ending the war the way he did. Okinawa had to decide it for him. It was a terrible fight and the losses were horrible, especially for the civilians. If we had invaded Japan, millions would have died.

The death toll at Okinawa was indeed huge. The Japanese death total was 221,933 of which 109,629 were soldiers. The remaining 112,304 deaths included civilians and forced laborers from Okinawa and Korea. U.S. casualties totaled 12,250 dead and 36,361 wounded. The total death toll of 234,183 exceeds Hiroshima and Nagasaki, combined, after the two atomic weapons were used. President Truman's decision to use atomic weapons was made with the Okinawa death figures in mind. An invasion of the Japanese homeland would have been tremendously costly for both sides.

My father hated war, yet he never criticized Truman's decision. *Truman's decision was like me praying for that one man to die but on a much bigger scale. I'm a life-long Republican, but I respect the man. I'm glad it all ended. He made the right choice.*

He took another "breather" and then continued. *It wasn't long after that I was sent home—for good. There was a point system for going home and I had way more points than needed.*

But before I left, the Executive Officer asked if I would stay. He said they'd put me in for Chief and then Warrant Officer. You know my Uncle Fred was a career Warrant—a double plank owner on the Yorktown. *Maybe they thought Navy careers would run in the family. They were wrong. I passed on the offer.*

At this point I was truly surprised. I knew that regardless of what negative things he had seen and experienced, he loved that ship and that time in his life. To learn that he could have stayed with a significant promotion and perhaps a career, and did not, was baffling to me. It was not what I expected. "Didn't you even think about staying?"

Not at all. I had served over five years, seen enough of the world—seen more than enough of other things. I was ready to come home. I wanted to come home.

Also included in the newspaper article that had described my father as a tight-lipped combat veteran home on leave, I found additional information to help understand his feelings. Its opening lines took readers back to the time of isolation when war was only a threat. It read: "People stopped to stare on the streets that January morning in 1941 when five Blue Island boys left for active duty. 'Where are you going?' said one of the onlookers. 'We're looking for a war,' countered one of the five."

Who made the comment? I never asked him. It could have been him, but I believe it makes no difference. The Chicago Boys found their war and for my father, it was now over.

PEACE PROCLAMATION

Representatives from the Allied Powers and Japan have just completed the signing of the terms of Surrender aboard the Battleship U.S.S. *Missouri* in Tokyo Bay—and so peace has officially been proclaimed again throughout the world.

While the official status of the peace is a cause for gratification in the thought of a job well done, there is still a great deal of work for the Navy to do. It is expected that the same spirit of accomplishment that has carried us to victory will manifest itself in our everyday tasks in the days to come.

On this V-J Day, let us observe a moment of silent prayer and thanksgiving to Almighty God. Let us remember with gratitude those of our comrades who gave their lives that this day might come. We pray that we may be worthy of their sacrifice and for courage and wisdom in the task of establishing and maintaining a just and righteous peace in the days that are ahead.

Second Division Officer, Lt. John Barrett, stands proud above *The Gangster's* score-board where seven verified kills of enemy planes are displayed.

Chapter 30

Tokyo Bay, At Last! – September 1945

By the time the *Fuller's* PLAN OF THE DAY FOR MONDAY, 3 SEP-TEMBER 1945, was posted and carried as its final item the preceding proclamation, my father was homeward bound—as a passenger on another vessel.

There were about two dozen of us that had so many points we could have gone home twice. That group was most of the original plank holders from the day we commissioned the Fuller. *The Navy transferred us to a ship headed home and we made it to San Francisco about two weeks after V-J Day. In San Francisco it was one big party, and it went on for some time. Everyone was relieved the war was over and they really celebrated.*

Home was so very different from being at sea. I learned that the Fuller *went on to Japan. By going home I missed getting a medal for the occupation of Japan. Several of the guys kept in touch and wrote to fill me in. I learned through their letters that the* Fuller *went as far as China.*

The semi-official account of the war's end for *The Gangster* follows:

> The end of the war saw us underway between Ulithi and our old blitzing grounds, Leyte. A great load was lifted from our minds, and it could not be long now before we would be home for good. Our passengers were debarked here, as well as the first contingent of men transferred home for discharge, who left the ship on August 27th. We then ran up to Manila, arriving there on the 29th of August. It was while we were anchored here that the final peace agreement was signed aboard the battleship *Missouri* in Tokyo Bay. We loaded with an Army detachment, and with our old division we got underway in company with TG 33.4, Japan bound. The group arrived in Tokyo Bay on the 13th of September and immediately

unloaded at the Yokohama docks, which had been thoughtfully left standing for us by the Army fliers. So here we are in Tokyo Bay as part of the Occupation Forces of Japan!

Although my grandmother, Harriet Staecker, marched against the war, she prominently positioned this picture for all entering her home to know she was proud of her sons' service. On the left, is my uncle Arthur Staecker, my father, Irvin Staecker is on the right. Standing behind them is their brother, Vernon Staecker.

THE LADY GANGSTER

Chapter 31

Lady Lost

My father had no reason to regret not seeing Japan or China as the *Fuller's* stays in both countries were brief and restricted to transport assignments. Her China trip was made, as usual, to deliver troops. On that occasion, the 1st Marine Division was aboard the *Fuller* again. Even in victory, the glorious old lady was put to task delivering her favorite Marines.

On October 4th, off of Tientsin, China, a second group of forty-nine "high point" men was transferred for return to the United States. With that move, all of the original Chicago Boys who had commissioned the ship at Lake Union in early 1941 had left *The Gangster*.

The *Fuller* completed her amazing journey in service to America and returned to Seattle on December 3rd, 1945. In five action-packed years, the aged passenger-cargo vessel had given her all in the global struggle known as World War II.

The semi-official account of the *Fuller's* exploits with the Chicago Boys ends with:

```
This story is finished, but the last chap-
ter(s) in the life of the U.S.S. Fuller are
yet to be written. It may be that she will
be returned to the merchant service to con-
tinue the peaceful life from which she was
so rudely jerked in 1940. Perhaps she will
be considered too old for further service
and will spend her remaining years quietly
in some secluded backwater. It is also pos-
sible that she will be retained in the
Navy…in the service that she has served so
faithfully for the past four-and-a-half
years, for in all, the Fuller has partici-
pated in the following war operations:
```

155

(1) Transporting units of the First Marine Division to Rejykavik, Iceland

(2) Transporting of American Expeditionary Force to Belfast, Northern Ireland

(3) Initial landing at Guadalcanal, Solomon Islands

(4) Reinforcement of Guadalcanal and consolidation of the Solomon Islands

(5) Initial assault of Bougainville, and the reinforcement of Bougainville

(6) Assault and occupation of Saipan, Marianas Islands

(7) Assault and occupation of Tinian, Marianas Islands

(8) Assault and occupation of Peleliu, Palau Islands

(9) Assault and occupation of Leyte, Philippine Islands

(10) Reinforcement of Leyte, Philippine Islands

(11) Assault and occupation of Luzon at Lingayen Gulf, Philippine Islands

(12) Reinforcement of Luzon at Lingayen Gulf, Philippine Islands

(13) Assault and occupation of Okinawa, Ryukus Islands

(14) Occupation of Japan!

Whatever her destiny, the old lady has a proud career to look back upon. She can point to that career, and say to the newer, faster, and technically better ships which

```
will take over her old job, "There you are,
ladies, try and beat it."
```

But neither continued service nor relaxed retirement was in store for one of the most battle-proven ships of World War II. The USS *Fuller* (APA-7), a.k.a. *The Gangster,* was decommissioned on March 20, 1946, and transferred to the Maritime Commission on July 1ˢᵗ of that year.

Although several official sources list her final disposition as "unknown," it has been reported by several crew members that the glorious old lady made her last call in a Portland, Oregon, shipyard in 1946. In 1957, she was cut up and sold as scrap.

Whatever information is the truth concerning the actual disposition of the physical entity known as the *Fuller* makes no real difference. What is important is the truth my father shared with me on our unforgettable journey.

As my father told me: *The ship is a real live being. She took on the personality of all the men who served on her. Mixed in the paint on her decks was the sweat and blood of a lot of boys from the Chicago-area reserves. The* Fuller *was, and always will be,* The Gangster. *The* Fuller *was us!*

Chapter 32

The End of the Ride

At the end of the war, my father came home to Blue Island, the town where he was raised. He had traveled much of the world, saw new, beautiful, and exotic places. Yet, rather than settle elsewhere, he came home to live in the community he had left on that cold day in 1941. When I was a child, four of the six homes on our block were owned by members of my father's high school class. And yes, they were all veterans.

My father pursued a personal life vastly different from the one he had led on *The Gangster*. He was a violinist, a Little League coach, a Scout Master, and a friend to the less fortunate. Our home became a way-station for hobos, down-on-their-luck relatives and friends, and immigrants of all faiths and colors.

During my time in the active duty Army, I was privileged to serve with two Medal of Honor recipients. When asked by another young officer what "the heroes" were like to be around, I told him, "They remind me of my dad."

My father was not as highly decorated as others for his service on the *Fuller*, but he did possess a similar quality as those other heroes. It was the ability to elevate others. G. K. Chesterton explained that rare human quality when he wrote, "The really great person is the person who makes every person feel great." I observed that trait in my father every day that I was with him.

Until our trip, I had been blind to what made him special. It often takes some peculiar occurrence to clear a son's vision of his father. Because of that trip, I became aware of how I had unconsciously patterned myself after him. I can only hope that one day I might be seen by others to be as compassionate and thoughtful as my father.

During one of my visits with my uncle, I was given more insight. My Uncle Art told me, "There should be a cabinet-level position for the one person in America who cares most about others. It's a rare gift to make people feel good about themselves. That was your father. At a dance, he'd pick a shy wallflower and swirl her about. On weekends, he'd visit shut-ins and widows. He often volunteered for thankless tasks at our church and in the community. He truly cared more about other people, and all of us are the better for knowing him. Look at you; he opened up to you at the right time. He was tough on you for years. But he let you be and grow and then, at the right moment, he knew when to become your friend. He was amazing."

I am truly thankful for that broken radio. I often go back to that special time.

****

We pulled into my grandmother's driveway after more than eighteen hours on the road. I was not the least bit tired and wished the trip was longer. I did not want the story to end. There *had* to be more.

When my father spoke of her, *The Gangster* was so real. When he described the Chicago Boys, I could imagine all of them on the deck of the *Fuller*. I could clearly see him as one of those courageous young sailors. I could also see him as a "Salt." For the first time in my life I had a real understanding of who he was. I also did not want our time together to end. As we got out of the car, I asked, "Dad, do you ever miss it?"

Sure, at times I do, but only the good parts. I try to forget the bad things, and most of the time I can. When the bad pops up, it's only the good memories that can push them away. The important thing is to remember that it's all in the past. Life is now. What you do here and now is where new memories will come from. Make good memories while you can.

"Thanks for telling me about it." I awkwardly put out my hand.

Thanks for listening. He took my hand and shook it, just like I had seen him do with other men. He then put his arm around my shoulder, and we walked up the driveway. He said: *Now, let's wake up your grandmother, have some breakfast, and go work on that house.*

It was one of the best walks of my life.

During subsequent years, my father and I kept talking, and we became very close. His sharing the story of *The Gangster* saved and then deepened our relationship. After being apart for any length of time, we would reconnect by talking about the ship, its crew, and their exploits. *The Gangster* served as the level bridge that kept our uneven lives linked.

At every opportunity I asked my father questions, jotted notes, and tucked his rich tales of the USS *Fuller* and its crew in my memory. I was fascinated by the ship. For me, *The Gangster* was indeed a living being. My father was always a sailor inside, and in a sailor's fashion he always referred to the *Fuller* as "she," so I naturally thought of her so. To me, the *Fuller* was always *The Lady Gangster*. In my dreams I walk her decks with the Chicago Boys and talk with my father. Her story was a siren call beckoning to be told, and I pray that I have done her and her brave crew justice.

And, by the way... We never fixed the radio.

Irvin Henry Staecker (1917-1983), as he appeared in 1945 after five years in service aboard the USS *Fuller*.

Epilogue

In 1983, my father passed away at age sixty-six, having lived for another sixteen years after our memorable trip. His heart condition was finally diagnosed as cardiomyopthia and was attributed to the bout with measles he described in his journal during February 1941.

Among his papers was found a reminder to place the accompanying poem in his Bible.

> The Lord is my Pilot, I shall not drift.
>
> He lighteth me across the dark waters.
>
> He steereth me in the deep channels.
>
> He keepeth my Log.
>
> He guideth me by the Star of Holiness for His name's sake.
>
> I shall dread no danger; for Thou art with me.
>
> Thy love and Thy care they shelter me.
>
> Thou preparest a harbor before me in the Homeland of Eternity.
>
> Thou anointest the waves with oil, my ship rideth calm.
>
> Surely sunlight and starlight shall favor me on the voyage
>   I take,
>
> And I will rest in the port of God forever.

A Sailor's Memoir

USS Fuller

History:

Heywood Class Transport

Keel laid in 1919 as S.S. *City of Newport News* at Bethlehem Steel Corp., Alameda, California, for the Baltimore Mail Lines

Acquired by the U.S. Navy, November 12, 1940

Commissioned USS *Fuller* (AP-14), Lake Union, Seattle, Washington, April 9, 1941

Re-designated as an Attack Transport (APA-7), February 1, 1943

Decommissioned, March 20, 1946

Transferred to U.S. Maritime Commission, July 1, 1946

Final Disposition, listed in some records as fate unknown, yet reported by crew members as disassembled for scrap, in Portland, Oregon, in 1957

Specifications:

Displacement – 8,000 tons (unloaded); 14,450 tons (loaded)

Length – 507 feet

Beam – 56 feet

Draft – 22 to 25 feet

Speed – 16 knots (crew members alleged 21 knots)

Crew Complement – 43 officers, 337 enlisted

Troop Accommodations – 60 officers, 818 enlisted

Cargo Capacity – 130,000 cubic feet, 2,400 tons

Propulsion - Geared turbine drive (9,500 horse power) to a single screw

Armament – One five-inch gun
Four three-inch guns
Two, twin 40mm anti-aircraft guns
Eight, single 20mm anti-aircraft guns

Awards and Citations:

Combat Action Ribbon
American Defense Service Medal (with Fleet Clasp)
American Campaign Medal
Europe-Africa-Middle East Campaign Medal
Asiatic-Pacific Campaign Medal (nine Battle Stars)
World War II Victory Medal
Navy Occupation Service Medal (for Japan)
Philippines Liberation Medal (two Stars)
China Service Medal

Campaigns/Operations, 1941-1945:

Transport of 1st Marine Division to Rejykavik, Iceland—1941
Transport of American Expeditionary Force to Belfast, Northern
    Ireland—1941
Transport of Civilian Refugees from British Isles—1941
Guadalcanal-Tulagi Landings—August 7, 1942
Capture and Defense of Guadalcanal—August 1942 to February 1943
Treasury-Bougainville Operation (assault and reinforcement)—
    November 1-8, 1943
Marianas Operation (capture and occupation of Saipan)—
    June 15-24, 1944
Tinian (capture and occupation)—July 24-25, 1944
Western Caroline Islands (capture and occupation of southern Palau
    Islands)—September 1944
Leyte Operation – (Assault, occupation and reinforcement)—
    October-November 1944
Luzon Operation – (Assault, occupation and reinforcement)—
    January 1945
Okinawa Operation (Assault and occupation of Okinawa)—
    April 1-9, 1945
Occupation of Japan
China Service

Significant Personal Decorations/Awards:

Captain P. S. Theiss, USN - Awarded the Navy Cross
Captain M.E. Eaton, USN - Awarded the Legion of Merit
Captain N.M. Pigman, USN - Awarded a Letter of Commendation,
  from the 7th Fleet

Enemy Engaged and Destroyed:

7 confirmed enemy aircraft brought down

Casualties

8 killed (5 crew, 3 embarked troops), 35 wounded, November 8, 1943

A Sailor's Memoir

Photo Credits

I wish to thank the following people and organizations who allowed me the use of their photographs:

Hennig, Richard R., a *Fuller* crewmember: Photo on page 34.

National World War II Museum, New Orleans, Louisiana: Photo on page 80.

Staecker, Dwight and Elsie Staecker Steadman: Photos on pages 22, 94, 95, 102, 107, 108, 152, 154 and 162.

www.Hyperwar.com: Photo of the painting used on the front cover, opposite the dedication page, on chapter headings; and the photo on page 9.

A Sailor's Memoir

Suggested Reading

There are many excellent books about World War II. The following titles are among those I found insightful concerning the Pacific Theater.

At Dawn We Slept: The Untold Story of Pearl Harbor
  - Gordon William Prange

Eagle Against the Sun: The American War with Japan - Ronald Spector

Guadalcanal: The Definitive Account of the Landmark Battle
  - Richard B. Frank

Guadalcanal Diary - Richard Tregaskis

With the Old Breed: At Peleliu and Okinawa - Eugene B. Sledge

Touched with Fire - Eric Bergerud

Flags of Our Fathers - James Bradley

American Caesar: Douglas MacArthur 1880-1964 - William Manchester

Nimitz - E. B. Potter

Bull Halsey - E. B.Potter

Fiction:

Away All Boats - Kenneth Dodson
  (the author of this novel served aboard an APA, the USS *Pierce*, 1943-45)

A Sailor's Memoir

THE LADY GANGSTER

Author Bio

Del Staecker, a former Army officer, received his Bachelor of Arts degree in history, from The Citadel. Additionally, he has studied history at Wheaton College, and the University of Puget Sound.

A Fellow of the Royal Society of Arts, he is now a full-time writer and the author of two novels: *The Muted Mermaid* and *Shaved Ice*. Staecker's third novel, *Chocolate Soup*, will be released in 2009.

Notes

Notes

Notes